Play Activities for the Early Years

Practical Ways to Promote Purposeful
Learning Across the Foundation Stage

Herjinder Uppal

Note

We have included publishers for all the children's books referred to in this book to enable you to get hold of them more easily. In many cases the book will have been published in a variety of formats (eg hardback and board book), sometimes by different publishers. We have not supplied publishers for traditional fairy tales (such as *The Three Little Pigs*) as there are so many versions available.

Published by Brilliant Publications
1 Church View, Sparrow Hall Farm, Edlesborough,
Dunstable, Bedfordshire LU6 2ES

Tel: 01525 229720
Fax. 01525 229725
email: sales@brilliantpublications.co.uk
website: www.brilliantpublications.co.uk

Written by Herjinder Uppal
Illustrated by Sarah Wimperis
Cover design by Lynda Murray

ISBN 1 903853 48 6
© Herjinder Uppal

First published in 2004
10 9 8 7 6 5 4 3 2 1

Printed in Malta by Interprint Ltd

Contents

Introduction

Play Activities for the Early Years provides over 100 activities to cover the entire Foundation Stage curriculum. The key theme of each activity is learning through play. Play is critical in the development of a child. Children are able to learn almost everything through play and their emotional, physical, social and creative development can be enhanced through quality play experiences. The activities presented in this book will enhance children's natural eagerness to learn and help them reach their full potential, whilst having a good time.

This book is aimed at early years practitioners working in a variety of settings including reception classes, nurseries, pre-schools, playgroups, childminding at home, and mother and toddler groups. The activity sheets can be used for a variety of purposes including:

◆ long-term and short-term curriculum planning
◆ assessment and record-keeping
◆ enabling classroom assistants and helpers to understand how best to carry out a task and how to participate in order to enhance the children's learning
◆ being placed next to displays of children's work to explain how it was produced and what the children learnt
◆ being given to parents to enhance their understanding of what and how their child is learning and to offer suggestions for them to build on at home.

A unique feature of this book is that it provides everything you would need to deliver a high quality curriculum for three to five year olds. It covers all the early learning goals and the different stepping stones. The activities can be used with children at different stages of their development and can also be easily modified to meet the needs of the children. An added advantage is that this book is concise and simple to use and will allow early years practitioners to plan day-to-day activities confidently in their classroom. The activities can be used methodically, or dipped into at any time throughout the year.

How to use this book

This book is made up of six chapters, one for each early learning goal.
Each chapter has a similar format including:

- ◆ an introduction to the chapter
- ◆ a learning opportunities table
- ◆ activity pages.

Chapter introduction

Each chapter begins with an introduction, highlighting the key skills and concepts that will be addressed in the chapter.

Learning opportunities table

In this table each early learning goal is broken down into specific learning opportunities. For each learning opportunity the activities that will help the children achieve that target are listed. The relevant page numbers are given in brackets. Finally there is a column for comments, which can be used for planning and assessment purposes. The learning opportunity tables are photocopiable.

Activity pages

Each activity page is set up in a similar format with the following headings:

- ◆ **You will need** – this lists the resources needed to carry out the activity
- ◆ **Group size** – the size of group the activity is suited to
- ◆ **What to do** – a step-by-step bullet-pointed explanation of how to carry out the activity
- ◆ **Extension activities** – extra activities to reinforce the chosen goals and provide links to other subject areas
- ◆ **What will the children learn?** – all the ways children will learn by carrying out the task
- ◆ **Links to early learning goals** – the specific learning opportunities the activity aims to meet.

Several activities have photocopiable sheets linked to them to either support or extend the activity. These are found after the relevant sheet.

Communication, Language and Literacy

The development of language is crucial to children's overall development as it affects most of the other areas of the curriculum. Children need to be encouraged to use language in a wide variety of ways: to express feelings and ideas, to give and find information, to recall the past and think about the future, and to create imaginary worlds.

The activities in this chapter help children to:

◆ use language and communication in a variety of ways
◆ learn about the shapes and sounds of words
◆ understand written language and appreciate stories, rhymes and information from books
◆ take steps towards becoming a writer.

The early learning goal of Communication, Language and Literacy is broken down into 19 learning opportunities, which are listed on the chart on the pages 8–9. Each learning opportunity is covered by between two and five activities that will help children achieve that target. The last column on the chart is for comments, which can be used for planning and assessment purposes.

Learning opportunities chart

Learning opportunity	Activities (and page numbers)	Comments
Enjoy listening to and using spoken and written language, and readily turn to it in their play and learning	Listening area (10); Toy telephone (11); Hospital home corner (12–13)	
Explore and experiment with sounds, words and texts	I Spy rhyming game (14); Picture story (15); Nursery rhymes (16–17); Spider poem (18)	
Listen with enjoyment and respond to stories, songs and other music, rhymes and poems and make up their own stories, songs, rhymes and poems	Listening area (10); Picture story (15); Spider poem (18); The wheels on the fire engine (19)	
Use language to imagine and recreate roles and experiences	Hospital home corner (12–13); Happy birthday (20)	
Use talk to organize, sequence and clarify thinking, ideas, feelings and events	Events of the day (21); Happy/sad masks (22–24); Copy my necklace (25)	
Sustain attentive listening, responding to what they have heard by relevant comments, questions or actions	Copy my necklace (25); Feely bag game (26)	
Interact with others, negotiating plans and activities and taking turns in conversation	What am I doing? (27–28); My friend's weekend (29); Favourite animals (30)	
Extend their vocabulary, exploring the meanings and sounds of new words	Nursery rhymes (16–17); Feely bag game (26); Food tasting (31); Finish the sentence (32)	
Retell narratives in the correct sequence, drawing on the language patterns of stories	Puppet theatre (33); Story of the week (34)	
Speak clearly and audibly with confidence and control and show awareness of the listener, for example by their use of conventions such as greetings, 'please' and 'thank you'	Toy telephone (11); Good manners certificate (35–36); Pass the teddy (37)	
Hear and say initial and final sounds in words, and short vowel sounds within words	Object game (38); Same sound (39); Snap (40–41)	
Link sounds to letters, naming and sounding the letters of the alphabet	Snap (40–41); Alphabet biscuits (42-43); Letter of the week (44)	

This page may be photocopied by the purchasing institution only.

Play Activities for the Early Years
www.brilliantpublications.co.uk

Learning opportunities chart

Learning opportunity	Activities (and page numbers)	Comments
Read a range of familiar and common words and simple sentences independently	Finish the sentence (32); Word lotto (45–46); Word search (47); Mixed up sentence (48); Making a book (49)	
Know that print carries meaning and, in English, is read from left to right and top to bottom	Favourite animals (30); Making a book (49); Books from around the world (50); Chocolate rice snaps cakes (51–52); Shopping at the supermarket (57–58)	
Show an understanding of the elements of stories, such as main characters, sequence of events and opening, and how information can be found in non-fiction texts to answer questions about where, who, why and how	Favourie animals (30); Puppet theatre (33); I am Goldilocks / Baby Bear (53–55); Book about me (56);	
Attempt writing for various purposes, using features of different forms such as lists, stories and instructions	Hospital home corner (12–13); Shopping at the supermarket (57–58); Mother's/Father's Day card (59–61)	
Write their own names and other things such as labels and captions and begin to form simple sentences, sometimes using punctuation	Finish the sentence (32); Mixed up sentence (48); Mother's/Father's Day card (59–61); Name t-shirt (62); Diary (63)	
Use their phonic knowledge to write simple regular words and make phonetically plausible attempts at more complex words	Book about me (56); Mother's/Father's Day card (59–61); Three-letter words (64–65)	
Use a pencil and hold it effectively to form recognizable letters, most of which are correctly formed	Letter of the week (44); Mother's/Father's Day card (59–61); Name t-shirt (62); Chopstick challenge (66)	

Play Activities for the Early Years
www.brilliantpublications.co.uk

This page may be photocopied by the purchasing institution only.

9

Listening area

You will need

An area set aside in the classroom; tape recorder; headphones; microphone; story and nursery rhyme tapes and corresponding books; musical instruments; telephone; blank tapes; puppets

What will the children learn?

◆ Listening skills, developed through a range of activities and resources
◆ To use a tape recorder independently
◆ To enjoy stories, rhymes and poems
◆ Creativity and imagination
◆ Role play – using the telephone and puppets

Group size

Small groups

What to do

◆ Explain to the children that you are going to create a listening area in the classroom.
◆ Ask the children to suggest the things they would like there.
◆ Use these suggestions to set up the area.
◆ Invite the children in small groups to use the area.
◆ Show children how to operate the tape recorder to not only listen to tapes but also record their own stories/poems/rhymes.
◆ Provide instruments so children can play and listen to the various sounds they make.
◆ Invite children to use puppets to retell stories and act out different scenarios.
◆ Provide telephones so children can pretend to ring each other and talk.
◆ Play with the children to model the type of language they should be using.

Extension activities

◆ Encourage the children to share stories with each other.
◆ Ask children to make puppets to use in the listening area (see Puppet theatre, page 33).
◆ Make instruments to play in the listening area.
◆ Ask children to tape record various outdoor sounds to listen to on the tape recorder.
◆ Set up a table of objects that make noises, such as bells or wind chimes.
◆ Ask children to hold a shell to their ear and describe what they can hear.

Links to early learning goals

◆ Enjoy listening to and using spoken and written language, and readily turn to it in their play and learning
◆ Listen with enjoyment and respond to stories, songs and other music, rhymes and poems and make up their own stories, songs, rhymes and poems

Toy telephone

You will need
Paper cups; string

Group size
Whole class, then in pairs

What to do

What will the children learn?
- Listening and speaking skills
- Working in pairs – cooperation and turn-taking
- Conversation skills
- How to cope in an emergency situation
- Good manners

- Show children how to make a toy telephone by tying a piece of string between two cups.
- Invite one child to put the cup to their ear and ask another child to stand so that the string is pulled tight and talk into the cup.
- Ask the children to explain how it sounds when the other child talks – now reverse roles and try again.
- Discuss the things people say when they talk on the telephone, for example: 'Hello, how are you?'
- Talk about the different people the children talk to on the telephone (eg Dad, Mum, cousins, friends). Do they talk to each person differently?
- Discuss how you would use the phone if there was an emergency. What number would you ring? How would you speak? What information would you need to supply?
- Invite the children to make their own phones using paper cups and string.
- Pair the children and ask them to pretend having different telephone conversations.
- Finish by displaying the phones so the children can use them during free play sessions.

Extension activities
- Play a pass the parcel game but with a phone – the person holding the phone when the music stops has to choose a friend to pretend to talk to on the phone.
- Explain how a phone works.
- Record some telephone conversations onto a tape and place them in the listening area so that the children can listen to them.

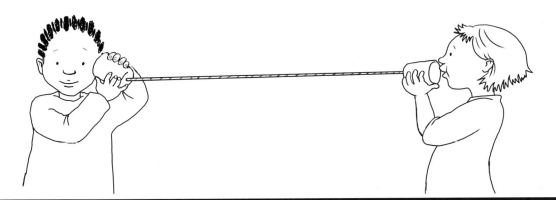

Links to early learning goals
- Enjoy listening to and using spoken language and readily turn to it in their play and learning
- Speak clearly and audibly with confidence and control and show awareness of the listener, for example by their use of conventions such as greetings, 'please' and 'thank you'

Hospital home corner

You will need

Labels for hospital home corner (see page 13); home corner set up as a hospital; doctor's uniform (for adult); toy doctor's case with stethoscope; thermometer, bandages, plasters, cotton wool, etc; medicine slips; note pad; telephone; willing adult helper

What will the children learn?

◆ Listening and speaking skills
◆ Role play
◆ To extend vocabulary and learn new words
◆ To attempt writing

Group size

Small groups

What to do

◆ Invite children to play in the hospital home corner.
◆ Ask the children to be patients while the adult helper pretends to be a doctor.
◆ The adult dresses up and acts like a doctor. Ensure they keep in character as this will motivate the children to play along.
◆ The adult can extend the children's vocabulary by introducing new words such as 'stethoscope', 'thermometer', and 'prescription'.
◆ Now reverse roles and encourage the children to use the new words.
◆ Invite the children to write out a prescription on a note pad.

Extension activities

◆ Invite a doctor/nurse in to talk to the children or take a trip to a doctor's surgery or hospital.
◆ Talk about how doctors and nurses help us.
◆ Discuss what children should do in an emergency.
◆ Show the equipment in a doctor's case and talk about how it is used.
◆ Read *Day in the Life of a Doctor* by Linda Hayward (Dorling Kindersley Publishing).

Links to early learning goals

◆ Enjoy listening to and using spoken and written language, and readily turn to it in their play and learning
◆ Use language to imagine and recreate roles and experiences
◆ Attempt writing for various purposes, using features of different forms such as lists, stories and instructions

Labels for home corner

doctor	nurse
patient	waiting room
surgery	receptionist
medicine	stethoscope
plasters	bandage
thermometer	x-ray

I Spy rhyming game

You will need
Flip chart and pens

Group size
Whole class

What will the children learn?
◆ Listening and speaking skills
◆ To understand what rhyming means and put it into practice

What to do
◆ Begin by explaining what rhyming means. Write some rhyming words on a flip chart, for example: 'cat rhymes with bat', 'ball rhymes with tall'.
◆ Now discuss how the I spy rhyming game is played – instead of saying, 'I spy something beginning with (a letter), the person has to say, 'I spy something that rhymes with (a word).'
◆ Play the I Spy rhyming game.
◆ Let children have turns at guessing and asking.

Extension activities
◆ Make an I Spy rhyming flap book.
◆ Read some nursery rhymes and ask children to make up their own rhymes.
◆ Count how many words they can think of which rhyme with 'cat' (or another word).
◆ Make up a class poem using rhyming.

Link to early learning goals
◆ Explore and experiment with sounds, words and texts

Picture story

You will need
Pictures of different objects
or actions

Group size
Large groups

What will the children learn?
- Listening and speaking skills – listening to each person carefully and continuing the story
- Story-telling as a group
- Imagination
- To use language patterns in stories

What to do
- Sit the children in a circle.
- Stack a pile of pictures in the middle.
- Explain to the children that they are going to make up a story using the pictures. Each child will say one sentence using the picture as a guide.
- Let the first child pick the top card and start the story. Help them if they find it difficult – make a suggestion. For example, if it is a picture of a boy, you could say, 'Once upon a time there was a boy called George.'
- Now the next child picks up the next card and continues the story. For example, if it is a picture of an apple, they could say, 'George loved eating apples.'
- Continue until all the children have had a turn and the last child finishes the story.
- Now shuffle the pictures and start again.

Extension activities
- Write down or tape record the stories.
- Instead of picture cards you could use objects.
- Make up a poem using the picture cards.
- Ask children to make their own picture cards by using small pieces of card and pictures cut out of magazines.
- Make picture cards of a story they know. See if the children can sequence the cards in the correct order.

Links to early learning goals
- Explore and experiment with sounds, words and texts
- Listen with enjoyment and respond to stories, songs and other music, rhymes and poems and make up their own stories, songs, rhymes and poems

Nursery rhymes

You will need

Teddy bear; mixed up nursery rhymes sheet (see page 17); scissors; glue; paper

Group size

Whole class, then small groups

What will the children learn?

◆ Listening and speaking skills – to listen to and continue a nursery rhyme
◆ To understand what a sentence is
◆ Rhyming words
◆ To sequence
◆ To memorize and recite nursery rhymes

What to do

◆ Begin by saying some nursery rhymes with the children.
◆ Show the children the teddy bear and explain that the only person who can speak is the person holding the teddy.
◆ Now say the first line of a nursery rhyme and then pass Teddy on to a child and ask if they can say the next line, and then they pass it on and so on until the nursery rhyme is complete.
◆ Show the children the sheet of nursery rhyme pictures which are in the wrong order.
◆ Ask them to cut out the pictures and arrange them in the right order.
◆ Stick the pictures onto paper.
◆ Finish the activity by letting the children share their work with the class and recite the rhyme.

Extension activities

◆ Give children dress up clothes and props and ask them to act out nursery rhymes.
◆ Make a book about the children's favourite nursery rhymes.
◆ Find out the children's favourite nursery rhymes and make a bar chart together.
◆ Use puppets to act out rhymes.

Links to early learning goals

◆ Explore and experiment with sounds, words and texts
◆ Extend their vocabulary, exploring the meanings and sounds of new words

Mixed up nursery rhymes sheet

Hey Diddle Diddle

Hickory Dickory Dock

Jack and Jill

This page may be photocopied by the purchasing institution only.

Spider poem

You will need

Poems and nursery rhymes about minibeasts (eg 'Incy Wincy Spider' as shown); flip chart and pens; large piece of paper

Group size

Whole class

What will the children learn?

◆ Group work and cooperation
◆ Listening and speaking skills
◆ Poetry work
◆ To extend vocabulary and learn new words

What to do

◆ Begin by reading 'Incy Wincy Spider' or other poems and nursery rhymes about minibeasts.
◆ Explain to children that you are all going to work together and make up a poem about a spider.
◆ Write the word 'spider' down the side of the page:

> s
> p
> i
> d
> e
> r

◆ Explain that each line will start with each letter. In other words, the first line will begin with 's', the second with 'p' and so on.
◆ Work with the children, taking their ideas and also introducing them to new words.
◆ Finish by reading the poem together.
◆ Choose some children to copy a line onto a large piece of paper shaped as a spider.
◆ Display for all to enjoy.

Extension activities

◆ Write a poem about another minibeast in the same fashion.
◆ Write a rhyme about spiders, for example:

> Spiders are small
> They like to crawl
> They eat bugs and
> Like to hide in rugs.

◆ Listen to a wide range of stories, songs and poems about spiders and other minibeasts.
◆ Use non-fiction books to find information about spiders.
◆ Make a spider out of junk material.

Links to early learning goals

◆ Explore and experiment with sounds, words and texts
◆ Listen with enjoyment and respond to stories, songs and other music, rhymes and poems and make up their own stories, songs, rhymes and poems

The wheels on the fire engine

You will need
Flip chart and pen; tape recorder and microphone

Group size
Whole class

What will the children learn?
◆ Listening and speaking skills
◆ To recite songs from memory
◆ To make up new songs
◆ To recognize the sounds of different objects

What to do
◆ Begin with the children singing the song 'The Wheels on the Bus'.
◆ Now explain to children they are going to change the song to 'The Wheels on the Fire Engine'.
◆ Ask children to think of the different parts of the fire engine and about the noise it makes. For example, you might come up with: horn (beep, beep), hose pipe (whoosh, whoosh), ladder (up and down), siren (nee, naw).
◆ Write the children's ideas on the flip chart.
◆ Now sing the song again but with the new words.
◆ Finish by recording the song onto a tape and placing it in the listening area for all to enjoy.

Extension activities
◆ Do different versions for different vehicles, for example: a bicycle, a truck or an ambulance.
◆ Adapt other popular songs.
◆ Sing and listen to other songs and make a song tape to play in the listening area.
◆ Make a bus or fire engine using cardboard boxes, chairs, etc.
◆ Talk about what children should do if there is a fire at school.
◆ Go for a trip to a fire station or invite firefighters to visit the school.

Link to early learning goals
◆ Listen with enjoyment and respond to stories, songs and other music, rhymes and poems and make up their own stories, songs, rhymes and poems

Happy birthday

You will need
Birthday cards; book:
Kipper's Birthday by Mike
Inkpen (Hodder Headline Ltd)

Group size
Large groups

> ### What will the children learn?
> ◆ Listening and speaking skills – listen to a story and talk about their birthday
> ◆ To reflect on past experiences
> ◆ To link stories to their own lives

What to do
◆ Read the story *Kipper's Birthday*.
◆ Use the book as a stimulus to talk to the children about birthdays.
  Show the children some birthday cards.
◆ Invite the children to take turns to describe how they celebrated their last birthday.
◆ Ask questions to encourage the children to talk as much as they can on the topic.

Extension activities
◆ Ask the children to make birthday cards for Kipper.
◆ Ask the children to draw a cake with the right number of candles for their age.
◆ Make a list of all the children's birthdays in each month.
◆ Make a bar chart using the list of children's birthdays in each month.
◆ For each child's birthday give a card and have a small celebration.
◆ Cook small birthday cakes.

> ### Link to early learning goals
> ◆ Use language to imagine and recreate roles and experiences

Events of the day

You will need

Photographs of children in the class doing different things in the day; paper; glue

Group size

Small groups

What will the children learn?
◆ To sequence events of the day
◆ Listening and speaking skills
◆ Group work and cooperation

What to do

◆ Show the children photos of the class doing different things during the day, for example arriving and taking off coats, snack time, etc.
◆ Ask the children to sort out the pictures and put them in the right order.
◆ Stick the pictures onto a large sheet of paper.
◆ Ask the group to show their work to the class and talk about the different events in the day.

Extension activities

◆ Ask children to talk about the things they did at the weekend starting on Saturday and finishing on Sunday.
◆ Give children pictures of activities they do in the morning (eg get out of bed, brush their teeth, eat breakfast). Ask the children to put the pictures in the correct sequence.
◆ Do time work. What time did we have our snack?
◆ Learn the days of the week and the months of the year.
◆ Give the children pictures of a story or nursery rhyme they know well. Ask them to put the pictures in the correct order (see Nursery rhymes, pages 16–17).

Link to early learning goals
◆ Use talk to organize, sequence and clarify thinking, ideas, feelings and events

Happy/sad masks

You will need

Happy mask (see page 23); Sad mask (see page 24). Photocopy the masks onto card and glue sticks to back as handles.

Group size

Whole class

What will the children learn?

◆ Listening and speaking skills – taking turns to speak and listen to others
◆ To express their emotions
◆ To review and look back on their day

What to do

◆ At the end of the day sit the children in a circle.
◆ Ask them to think how they feel their day has gone.
◆ Show them the happy and sad masks.
◆ Go round the circle and ask the children to choose the mask that shows their feelings and to explain why.
◆ You can start by saying how you feel, for example: 'I chose the happy mask because I enjoyed playing in the home corner with John and Sunita.'

Extension activities

◆ Make masks to represent other emotions: angry, excited, surprised, etc.
◆ Ask children to make some masks using different resources.
◆ Show masks from other cultures, for example Chinese, African or Indian masks.
◆ Have a quiet area where children can go if they feel sad or angry.
◆ Make a list of all the things that make them happy/sad.

Link to early learning goals

◆ Use talk to organize, sequence and clarify thinking, ideas, feelings and events

Play Activities for the Early Years
www.brilliantpublications.co.uk

Happy mask

23

Sad mask

Play Activities for the Early Years
www.brilliantpublications.co.uk

Copy my necklace

You will need
Keys, rings, beads and buttons of different shapes and colours (two of each); string; large piece of thick card

What will the children learn?
◆ To listen carefully and follow instructions
◆ To ask questions
◆ Fine motor control – threading

Group size
Pairs

What to do
◆ Sit two children at a table.
◆ Use the card to make a screen between the children. Make sure that they cannot see each other.
◆ Give each child a string and one of each of the items. For younger children limit the number of items.
◆ Now ask just one child to string the objects on their string and tie a knot at each end when they have finished.
◆ Ask the child with the necklace to give instructions to the other child so that they put objects on their necklace in the same sequence. For example, 'Put the key on first, now put on the yellow, round bead.'
◆ The other child can ask questions to check they are following the instructions correctly.
◆ When finished remove the screen and compare the necklaces.

Extension activities
◆ Use the same technique for other activities, for example making models, pictures, etc.
◆ Blindfold one child and ask another child to give directions so that the child can walk from one side of the classroom to the other safely.
◆ Pretend one child is a robot and another child has to give it instructions to do a certain activity (see Robot game, page 95).
◆ Play games in which the children have to listen carefully, such as Simon Says.

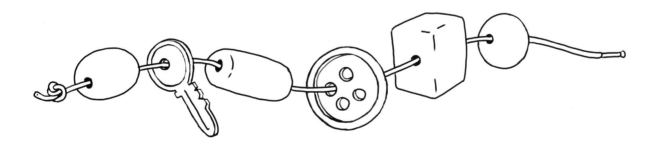

Links to early learning goals
◆ Use talk to organize, sequence and clarify thinking, ideas, feelings and events
◆ Sustain attentive listening, responding to what they have heard by relevant comments, questions or actions

Feely bag game

You will need

Large bag; different objects (eg teddy bear, keys, cup, book, iron and pen)

Group size

Large groups

What will the children learn?

◆ To ask and answer questions
◆ Listening and concentration skills
◆ Tactile ability – learning through touch

What to do

◆ Place an object in the bag without the children seeing.
◆ Explain to the children that they are going to take turns to guess what an object is by just feeling it. Explain that they should not tell anyone what they think the object is.
◆ The other children have to ask questions to find out what the object is. For example, 'Is it small?' 'Is it used in the house?' The child with the bag can answer only 'yes' or 'no'.
◆ Limit the children to 10 questions.
◆ Encourage the children to listen carefully to each other's answers to help them ask their next question.
◆ Finish by asking the children to guess what the object is. Check to see if they are correct.
◆ Ensure all the children have turns being both the feeler and the questioner.

Extension activities

◆ Play a yes/no game. One child pretends to be someone famous and the other children have to ask questions to guess who they are.
◆ Play Chinese Whispers. See if the message at the end is the same as the one at the beginning.
◆ Play card games such as Patience or Snap to build concentration.
◆ Invite a speaker in (according to the topic of the term). Ask the children to be respectful and listen carefully. Encourage them to think of and ask relevant questions.

Links to early learning goals

◆ Sustain attentive listening, responding to what they have heard by relevant comments, questions or actions
◆ Extend their vocabulary, exploring the meanings and sounds of new words

What am I doing?

You will need
What am I doing? sheet (see page 28)

Group size
Large groups

What will the children learn?
◆ To use different ways of communicating
◆ Gross motor skills – use body to convey information
◆ Group cooperation – turn-taking

What to do
◆ Show the children the What am I doing? sheet. Discuss the various activities shown.
◆ Explain to the children that you are going to act out one of the activities and you want them to guess which one you are doing.
◆ Now ask the child who guessed correctly to choose a different activity from the sheet and to act it out for the others to guess.
◆ Carry on until all the children have had a turn at miming.

Extension activities
◆ Ask children to make facial expressions to convey how they are feeling.
◆ Play Chinese Whispers, but instead of a whisper, pass round a gesture such as a wink or a pat on the back.
◆ Ask the children to use puppets to retell a story (see Puppet theatre, page 33).
◆ Show the children a collection of different foods. Ask one child to mime eating one of the foods for the other children to guess which one they are eating.
◆ Give the children a safety mirror and ask them to make different facial expressions.

Link to early learning goals
◆ Interact with others, negotiating plans and activities and taking turns in conversation

What am I doing? sheet

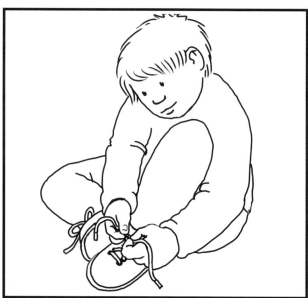

This page may be photocopied by the purchasing institution only.

Play Activities for the Early Years
www.brilliantpublications.co.uk

My friend's weekend

You will need
No special requirements

Group size
Pairs

What will the children learn?
◆ To work collaboratively
◆ Cooperation skills
◆ Listening and speaking skills – listening to someone and then sharing this with someone else

What to do
◆ Ask the children to sit in pairs facing each other.
◆ Explain to the children that you would like them to talk to one another about the things they did that weekend.
◆ Point out that they only have a minute each to talk and find out as much information as possible. Encourage the children to question their partner to get as much information as possible.
◆ Once they have finished ask each child to report back what their partner did.

Extension activities
◆ Ask the children to talk to each other about different topics, for example their family or their favourite holiday.
◆ Invite children to share a book with a partner (eg an older child or adult).
◆ Ask children to copy each other's body movements.
◆ Provide musical instruments. Ask one child to play a sound pattern for the other child to copy.

 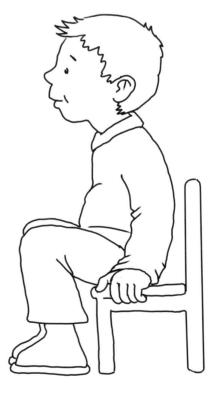

Link to early learning goals
◆ Interact with others, negotiating plans and activities and taking turns in conversation

Favourite animals

You will need
Older children; reference books about animals; paper and pen

Group size
Pairs

What will the children learn?
◆ Group cooperation
◆ That information can be gained from books
◆ To recognize non-fiction books and their purpose
◆ To name the key features of a non-fiction book
◆ To use new words about books and animals

What to do
◆ Begin by discussing the difference between non-fiction and fiction books.
◆ Explain that the purpose of a non-fiction book is to provide information.
◆ Go through the features of a non-fiction book: contents page, index, etc.
◆ Ask children what their favourite animal is and why.
◆ Divide the children into pairs. Where possible put younger children with older ones.
◆ Ask them to work together to find out some information about their animal using the non-fiction books provided.
◆ Finish with each pair talking to the class about the information they gathered.
◆ Ask the children if they found out something that they did not know before.

Extension activities
◆ The children could make reference books about their favourite animal. They may need an older child or adult to help them.
◆ Make a book about favourites, for example: 'My favourite colour', 'My favourite food'.
◆ When reading a non-fiction book ask the children to find the contents page and index.
◆ Ask the children to find books about other topics being studied.

Links to early learning goals
◆ Interact with others, negotiating plans and activities and taking turns in conversation
◆ Know that print carries meaning
◆ Understand how information can be found in non-fiction texts to answer questions about where, who, why and how

Play Activities for the Early Years
www.brilliantpublications.co.uk

Food tasting

You will need
A variety of food (jelly, sweets, lemon, noodles, apple, samosas, yoghurt)

Group size
Small groups

What will the children learn?
◆ New words for describing
◆ The different tastes of food – salty, spicy, sweet
◆ About food from different countries

What to do
◆ Before starting the activity check for food allergies and dietary requirements.
◆ Show the children a wide range of food.
◆ Invite the children to taste one of the foods, for example the jelly.
◆ Ask the children to describe how it feels in their mouth and also how it tastes.
◆ Do the same with the other food items.
◆ Model language by tasting some food yourself. For example, if you are eating a samosa you might say, 'It tastes spicy and it feels crunchy in my mouth.'

Extension activities
◆ Blindfold the children. Does it make a difference to how the foods taste?
◆ Cook food for tasting.
◆ Learn about the different areas of the tongue. There are only four different flavours we can taste – sour, salty, bitter and sweet. The front of the tongue tastes sweet flavours, the sides taste sour and the back is for bitter flavours. Salty flavours can be tasted all over the mouth.
◆ Have an international food day. Ask children to taste food from around the world (see International food, page 128).
◆ Make a bar chart of the children's favourite foods.

Link to early learning goals
◆ Extend their vocabulary, exploring the meanings and sounds of new words

Finish the sentence

You will need

Flip chart and pens; bag of descriptive words written on card (eg 'big', 'small', 'fierce', 'happy'); exercise books; pencils

Group size

Large groups

What will the children learn?
◆ New words for describing
◆ To understand the structure of a sentence and the need for punctuation
◆ To attempt to write simple sentences

What to do

◆ Write the start of a simple sentence on the flip chart and read it together. For example, 'The dog is ____'. Leave the end of the sentence blank.
◆ Ask one child to pick a word from a bag of descriptive words.
◆ Now write in the word to finish the sentence and read it together: 'The dog is <u>fierce</u>.'
◆ Talk to them about putting a full stop at the end to finish the sentence.
◆ Now do it again but choose a different ending.
◆ Older children could copy the sentence from the flip chart into their exercise books and then finish it with a word from the bag.
◆ Invite some of the children to try to read the sentences they have written.

Extension activities

◆ Use some nonsense endings, for example, 'The dog is blue.'
◆ Ask children to come up with some other descriptive words.
◆ Display a cut-out of a dog and ask the children to fasten the sentences on to it with Blu-tack®.
◆ Cut up the words in a sentence and ask the children to place them in order to form the sentence again.
◆ Invite the children to use the cut-up words they know to form other simple sentences.

Links to early learning goals

◆ Extend their vocabulary, exploring the meanings and sounds of new words
◆ Read a range of familiar and common words and simple sentences independently
◆ Write their own names and other things such as labels and captions and begin to form simple sentences, sometimes using punctuation

Puppet theatre

You will need

Book: *The Three Little Pigs*; chairs and blanket (for puppet theatre); old socks; felt-tip pens; pipe cleaners; felt; wool; fabric pieces; buttons; glue

What will the children learn?

◆ Creativity and imagination in art work
◆ To listen to and memorize a story
◆ To retell a story
◆ To act in character

Group size

Large groups

What to do

◆ Begin by reading the story *The Three Little Pigs*.
◆ Explain to the children that they are going to make puppets of the characters in the story (eg the three pigs, man that sells straw, sticks and bricks, and the wolf).
◆ Give the children the resources and let them create the puppets themselves.
◆ Set up a puppet theatre by draping the blanket over some chairs. The children can then hide behind the blanket and raise their hands so that the audience can see the puppets.
◆ Explain to the children that they are going to retell the story using the puppets.
◆ Encourage the children to change their voices to go with the puppet.
◆ Finish by showing the puppet play to another class.

Extension activities

◆ If possible, go to see a puppet show or invite a puppet show to the setting. This will give the children lots of ideas and also inspire them.
◆ Talk about the different ways and different resources used to make puppets.
◆ Use a puppet to represent one character from the story. Ask children to retell the story from that character's point of view. For example, the wolf might say: 'I was just so hungry but the pig wouldn't let me in.'
◆ Make puppets to go with other stories.
◆ Plan a birthday party for your puppets, then hold the party.
◆ Hide a puppet and give directions to a child to find it.
◆ Look at puppets from around the world.

Links to early learning goals

◆ Retell narratives in the correct sequence, drawing on the language patterns of stories
◆ Show an understanding of the elements of stories, such as main characters, sequence of events and openings

Story of the week

You will need

Storybook; dressing-up clothes and props

Group size

Whole class, then small groups

What will the children learn?

◆ To listen to and memorize a story
◆ To retell a story

What to do

◆ Choose a story of the week.
◆ Read the story out a few times over the week. Hopefully by the end of the week the children will be able to read it with you.
◆ When the children are familiar with the story, pause at different stages when reading the book and ask the children what happens next.
◆ Ask the children to retell the story to the class.
◆ Set up a display of the book and some dressing-up clothes and props.
◆ Invite children to act out the story, using the clothes and props, during free play.
◆ Make a wall display about the book and other activities based on it.

Extension activities

◆ Read a big book version of the story.
◆ Make some props to go with the story.
◆ Make puppets so children can use them to retell the story.
◆ Write out some words used in the story and see if the children can read them by sight.
◆ Make a magnetic story board with pictures of the characters (place a self-adhesive magnetic strip on the back of the pictures). Ask children to retell the story using the pictures.

Link to early learning goals

◆ Retell narratives in the correct sequence, drawing on the language pattern of stories

Good manners certificate

You will need
Good manners certificate (see page 36); chart with children's names on it; star stickers

Group size
Whole class

What will the children learn?
◆ Good manners
◆ To listen to each other
◆ To speak politely
◆ Respect for themselves and others
◆ To develop a positive atmosphere in the classroom

What to do
◆ Talk to the children about what good manners means, for example saying 'please' and 'thank you'.
◆ Ask the children to give examples of how they could use good manners in school, for example listening to others or talking politely.
◆ Explain to the children that every time the teacher or classroom assistant notices a child being a good talker or listener then they will get a star next to their name. The person who has the most stars at the end of the week will get the certificate.
◆ At the end of the week reward the 'Good manners certificate' to the winner.

Extension activities
◆ Instead of receiving a certificate, the pupil with the most stars at the end of the week could have their photograph displayed.
◆ Invite some people to talk to the group. Talk to the children beforehand about how they should greet the speakers and talk to them.
◆ Put some toy telephones in the home corner and ask children to hold pretend conversations with people (see Toy telephone, page 11). Discuss the different people they might talk to and how they can be polite.
◆ Make a list of good manners with the children (see Golden rules, page 181).
◆ Write a story about a child who was bad mannered and what happened to them.
◆ Read the story *The Bad-Tempered Ladybird* by Eric Carle (Puffin Books).

Link to early learning goals
◆ Speak clearly and audibly with confidence and control and show awareness of the listener, for example by their use of conventions such as greetings, 'please' and 'thank you'

Good manners certificate

This certificate is presented to

_____

for being a good talker and listener.

Well done!

 Play Activities for the Early Years
www.brilliantpublications.co.uk

Pass the teddy

You will need
Teddy bear

Group size
Small groups

What will the children learn?
◆ To say their own name and the names of other children
◆ Listening and speaking skills
◆ To cooperate in a familiar group
◆ To use the words 'please' and 'thank you'

What to do
◆ Ask the children to sit in a circle.
◆ Explain to the children that they are going to play a game to show they remember their friends' names.
◆ You hold the teddy and say, 'I am (your name).' Then pass the teddy to the child sitting next to you, saying, 'Hello (child's name), please will you look after the teddy?'
◆ The child takes the teddy and says, 'Thank you, (sender's name), of course I will look after it.' They then continue with, 'I am (name),' before passing the teddy to the next child and inviting them to look after it, as before.
◆ Continue around the circle until the teddy is back to you.

Extension activities
◆ Ask children to bring toys from home. Ask the children to swap toys. Have the children start by saying, 'I am (name), this is my toy.' Then swap it with a friend whist saying '(name of child) please will you look after my toy?' (See My favourite toy, page 174.)
◆ Do the same activity but use a ball which they can roll to the person of their choice.
◆ Invite speakers to the classroom. Remind the children that they need to talk politely and clearly.

Link to early learning goals
◆ Speak clearly and audibly with confidence and control and show awareness of the listener, for example by their use of conventions such as greetings, 'please' and 'thank you'

Object game

You will need
Various objects from home and school; pack of cards with letters of the alphabet on them

Group size
Large groups

What will the children learn?
◆ Letter names and sounds
◆ To link letter sounds to words
◆ To look at initial and final letter sounds in words

What to do
◆ Sit the children in a circle.
◆ Place a variety of objects in the middle of the circle.
◆ Mix up the alphabet cards and place them in a pile.
◆ Ask one child to pick the top card and say the letter name and sound. For younger children limit the number of cards.
◆ Now ask them, to pick an object beginning with that letter from the objects in the middle.
◆ Go round the circle doing the same for each child.

Extension activities
◆ Ask the children to pick a child's name that begins with the letter they have picked.
◆ Ask the children to pick the object first and then say the letter sound.
◆ Record letter sounds on tape so children can listen to and practise the sounds themselves.
◆ Cut out some pictures and ask children to write the letter sound of the object on the reverse.
◆ Write a sentence and ask children to circle how many of a certain letter sound they can see in it. Are they at the beginning, middle or end of the word?
◆ Play the game again, but this time ask the children to choose an object ending with the sound of the letter they have chosen.

Link to early learning goals
◆ Hear and say initial and final sounds in words, and short vowel sounds within words

Same sound

You will need
Paper; pencil; magazines; scissors; glue

Group size
Small groups

What will the children learn?
◆ To know which letters represent some of the sounds
◆ To hear and say initial and last letter sounds in words
◆ To write their name – be aware of the initial and final letter sounds in their name
◆ Fine motor skills – cutting with scissors

What to do
◆ Give each child a sheet of paper and ask them to write their name at the top of the paper. You may need to scribe for some children.
◆ Ask the children which letter is at the beginning of their name.
◆ Now give the children magazines and ask them to find pictures of things beginning with the same letter as at the beginning of their name.
◆ Ask the children to cut out the pictures they find and stick them onto the sheet of paper.
◆ Give the children another sheet of paper and write their name at the top as before.
◆ This time ask them which letter comes at the end of their name.
◆ Ask them to look in the magazines and find pictures beginning with that letter, and to cut them out and stick them on the paper.

Extension activities
◆ Break down the child's name into separate letters and ask the children to draw a picture to go with each letter. For example, for 'Tom' the child could draw a tomato, an orange and some milk.
◆ Play I Spy.
◆ Record a tape of letter sounds which children can listen to in the listening area.
◆ Link actions to letter sounds so children can say and remember them. For example, for the letter 's' the children could do the actions of a snake whilst saying the sound. There are a number of phonic reading schemes which suggest actions, for example Jolly Phonics.
◆ Write the children's names with some letters missing, for example E_ily. Ask the children to work out the missing letter.

Link to early learning goals
◆ Hear and say initial and final sounds in words, and short vowel sounds within words

Snap

You will need
Snap cards (see page 41).
Photocopy onto card and cut up
to produce two sets of cards.

Group size
Pairs

What will the children learn?
◆ Letter names and sounds
◆ To hear the initial sounds in words
◆ Sorting and matching skills
◆ Letter recognition and word knowledge

What to do
◆ Ask children to work in pairs, to play Snap.
◆ Give each child a set of cards.
◆ Each player takes it in turn to put down a card. If the pictures on the cards start with the same letter sound (eg 'bed' and 'banana'), then the children need to call out 'Snap'.
◆ Continue playing until either one player is out, or one player has all the cards.
◆ Now play a matching game.
◆ Spread out the cards on the table, face down.
◆ Ask each child to turn over one card and try to find another card with the same initial letter.
◆ Continue playing until all the cards are matched. The winner is the player with the most cards.

Extension activities
◆ Make a tape of letter names and sounds for the listening area. For example, 'The letter 'A' makes an 'a' sound,' (try to say just the letter sound and avoid saying 'uh' after the sound).
◆ Ask children to say the initial letter sounds in their name and the names of their friends.
◆ Ask children to think of things that begin with the same letter as at the beginning of their name (see Same sound, page 39).
◆ Do a letter sound for the week (see Letter of the week, page 44).
◆ Play with software packages on the computer which look at letters and letter sounds.

Links to early learning goals
◆ Link sounds to letters, naming and sounding the letters of the alphabet
◆ Hear and say initial and final sounds in words, and short vowel sounds within words.

Snap cards

Alphabet biscuits

You will need

Alphabet biscuits recipe (see page 43); ingredients for biscuits (see sheet); aprons; plastic knives or alphabet cutters

What will the children learn?

◆ Letter names, sounds, shapes and formation
◆ To develop their tactile ability – learning through touch
◆ To put together letter sounds to make words

Group size

Small groups

What to do

◆ Start by asking the children to wash their hands and put on aprons.
◆ Read the recipe together and make up the biscuit mixture. Roll out the dough.
◆ Ask the children to use alphabet cutters or plastic knives to cut out some letters from the dough. Talk about the shapes of the letters.
◆ Ask the children to use the letters to make a simple word.
◆ Remind them to think of letter sounds when forming the words.
◆ Bake the biscuits and let them cool.
◆ Encourage the children to feel the shape of the letters.
◆ Finish by letting the children eat their words.

Extension activities

◆ Bake cakes and use icing to write words on top.
◆ Ask the children to write their name using biscuit letters.
◆ Make letters out of different materials: playdough, paper, clay, etc.
◆ Encourage the children to play games with wooden and plastic letters. For example, ask the children to put the letters in alphabetical order.
◆ Use letter stencils to write their name and other simple words.

Link to early learning goals

◆ Link sounds to letters, naming and sounding the letters of the alphabet

Alphabet biscuits recipe

You will need

100 g (4 oz) of butter

50 g (2 oz) of sugar

150 g (6 oz) of flour

bowl

wooden spoon

sieve

rolling pin

baking tray

What to do

1. Preheat the oven to 150°C/ 300°F/ gas mark 2.

2. Beat the butter and sugar together.

3. Sieve the flour.

4. Add the flour to the butter and sugar mixture.

5. Use hands to form a dough.

6. Roll out the dough.

7. Make letter shapes using alphabet cutters or a plastic knife.

8. Place the biscuits on a greased baking tray and put in the oven for 20 minutes.

Letter of the week

You will need

Objects beginning with the letter of the week; paper; magazines; scissors; glue; pencils

Group size

Whole class

What will the children learn?
◆ Letter names and sounds
◆ To write letters

What to do

◆ Choose a letter for the week and do a variety of activities to reinforce the letter's sound and formation.
◆ Show children how to write the letter and talk about the sound it makes.
◆ Bring in some objects beginning with the letter. Show them to the children and put on a display table.
◆ Give each child a sheet of paper and some magazines. Ask them to cut out and stick some pictures of things beginning with the letter of the week.
◆ Ask children to practise writing the letter. Ensure that they hold pencils correctly and form the letter correctly.
◆ Finish by playing an I Spy game using only the letter of the week.

Extension activities

◆ Make a class scrap book of letters. Use collage materials to form letters and draw pictures of things beginning with the letter.
◆ Choose a letter sound or even word of the week.
◆ Make things in art that begin with the letter, for example: a spiral card snake for 's', a puppet for 'p', a butterfly picture for 'b'.
◆ Give each child a page from a magazine. Ask them to circle all the letters of the week they can find and to count how many.
◆ Make a list of words that the children can think of beginning with the letter and count them.

Links to early learning goals
◆ Link sounds to letters, naming and sounding the letters of the alphabet
◆ Use a pencil and hold it effectively to form recognizable letters, most of which are correctly formed

Word lotto

You will need

Word lotto cards (see page 46);
counters. Photocopy the sheet
twice onto card. Cut one sheet
along the thick lines to make
four boards. Cut the other sheet to make 24
individual word cards.

What will the children learn?
◆ To recognize and read common words
◆ Matching skills

Group size

Small groups

What to do

◆ Give each child a lotto board.
◆ Place a stack of word cards in the middle of the table.
◆ Invite the children to pick a card in turn.
◆ Help them to try to read the word.
◆ Ask them to try to match the word to one of the words on their sheet.
◆ If the child has that word on their sheet they put a counter on it.
◆ Now it is the next child's turn.
◆ Carry on until someone wins by covering all of the words on their sheet with counters.

Extension activities

◆ Make two sets of word cards and play Snap.
◆ Use cards to play matching and sorting games.
◆ Use the words to make simple sentences. Encourage children to try to sound out any words
  they are unsure of.
◆ Ask children to try to read the words independently.

Link to early learning goals
◆ Read a range of familiar and common words and simple sentences independently

Word lotto cards

are	the	he	no
I	go	Dad	cat
Mum	it	a	in
yes	play	dog	me
is	to	on	see
am	for	look	up

Play Activities for the Early Years
www.brilliantpublications.co.uk

Word search

You will need
Newspaper page – enlarged; common words (that the children have been learning) written on card (you could use page 46); pens

What will the children learn?
◆ To understand the concept of a word
◆ That print carries meaning
◆ To recognize and read common words
◆ To develop visual discrimination and concentration

Group size
Large groups

What to do
◆ Begin by going through the word cards. Read the words together.
◆ Now give each child one word card and an enlarged copy of a newspaper page.
◆ Ask children to find their word in the newspaper print and to circle it.
◆ Finish by asking the children to count how many words they found.
◆ See who found the most words and who found the fewest.

Extension activities
◆ Do the same activity but look for a letter rather than a word.
◆ Make cards of other common words. Use them to play various games, such as Snap.
◆ Display common words so they are available for children to refer to every day.
◆ Whilst reading a book ask children to read the words they know.
◆ Write two sentences that are identical except for one word. Ask the children to spot the difference.

Link to early learning goals
◆ Read a range of familiar and common words and simple sentences independently

Mixed up sentence

You will need
Strips of paper; pencils; scissors; glue; workbooks (or paper)

Group size
Small groups, then individually

What will the children learn?
◆ To read simple words
◆ To put together words to form a sentence
◆ To write simple words using correct pencil position and letter formation

What to do
◆ Ask a child to give you a sentence about what they like to do while at the setting. For example, 'I like to play football.'
◆ Write the sentence on a strip of paper.
◆ Now ask the child to read it with you.
◆ Cut up the sentence into separate words.
◆ Ask the child to put the words back into the correct order to make a sentence again.
◆ Let the children stick the words into their workbooks (or on a sheet of paper). Older children could be asked to write the sentence themselves underneath.
◆ Point out to the children the use of a capital letter at the beginning and a full stop at the end. Encourage them to use punctuation in their writing.

Extension activities
◆ Write a sentence but miss off the ending. Ask children to add different endings (see Finish the sentence, page 32).
◆ Ask the children to count how many words they can read.
◆ Write the children's names and then cut up the letters and use them to make other words.
◆ Ask children to try to read their friends' name.
◆ Each morning ask the children to write their name on the board, next to the activity they would like to do. Younger children could stick a card with their name on it next to their chosen activity.

Links to early learning goals
◆ Read a range of familiar and common words and simple sentences independently
◆ Write their own names and other things such as labels and captions and begin to form simple sentences, sometimes using punctuation

Making a book

You will need

Photos of each child in the class doing a variety of activities; hole punch; ribbon; pencil; pieces of card

Group size

Small groups

What will the children learn?
◆ To recognize the key features of a book
◆ To know books provide information
◆ Listening and speaking skills
◆ To read and write their name
◆ To build self-esteem and feel positive about themselves

What to do

◆ As a group look at books and discuss the key features such as cover, words, pictures and author.
◆ Explain to the children that they are each going to make a book about themselves.
◆ Look and talk about the children's photos together.
◆ Ask each child to choose five photos for their book.
◆ Stick each photo onto a piece of card.
◆ Ask the child what they would like you to write for each picture and scribe for them.
◆ On each card write a simple sentence, always using the child's name first. For example, 'John is sleeping,' or 'John is eating.'
◆ Make a cover for the book.
◆ Hole punch each card.
◆ Use a ribbon to bind the pieces of card together.
◆ Finish the activity by reading the books together and then display them in a prominent place.

Extension activities

◆ Ask more able children to form the sentences themselves using words they already know. Encourage them to sound out more complex words and attempt to write them themselves.
◆ Cut up the sentences and ask children to put in the correct order.
◆ Make the book using different materials. For example, you could make a zig-zag book by folding a long sheet of paper.
◆ Talk about fiction and non-fiction books and the differences. (See Book about me, page 56, where the children make a non-fiction book about themselves.)
◆ Work as a class and make up a story which can be made into a large book for shared reading.

Links to early learning goals
◆ Read a range of familiar and common words
◆ Know that print carries meaning and, English, is read from left to right and top to bottom

Books from around the world

You will need

Books from different cultures (eg Arabic books – books read from 'back' to 'front' and lines from right to left, Chinese books – print is read top to bottom and from right to left, English books – read from top to bottom and left to right)

What will the children learn?

◆ To recognize the key features of the books they read
◆ To notice similarities and differences between books they read and those from different cultures
◆ To see different scripts
◆ To appreciate diversity in the world

Group size

Large groups

What to do

◆ Talk to the children about the books in the classroom. Talk about how they hold the book and how they read and look at the pictures.
◆ Introduce words such as 'title', 'author', 'illustrator' and explain their meaning.
◆ Show how the book is read from top to bottom and left to right. Read a page using your finger to show where you are reading from.
◆ Now show them books from different cultures.
◆ Invite the children to look at how different languages are written.
◆ Talk about how the books are read. For example, explain that the front of an Arabic book is where we have the back, and that the back is where we have the front.
◆ Point out the different scripts.
◆ Finish by displaying the books in the reading corner for the children to explore themselves.

Extension activities

◆ Invite people from different communities to visit the setting and show how they read the books.
◆ Ask the children to attempt to write in different languages.
◆ Show the children alphabets in different languages. Count how many letters are in each.
◆ Ask the children to try to make an Arabic book – front on the right, back on the left.
◆ Invite the children to make their own picture story book. Show them where to write their name as author/illustrator.
◆ Whilst reading books ask children to point to the title, author and illustrator.
◆ Show the children authors' dedications in books. Children find this really interesting.

Link to early learning goals
◆ Know that print carries meaning and, in English, is read from left to right and top to bottom

Chocolate rice snaps cakes

You will need

Chocolate rice snaps cakes recipe (see page 52); aprons; ingredients for cakes (see sheet)

Group size

Small groups

What will the children learn?
◆ To understand that information can be relayed in print
◆ To follow instructions
◆ Basic cooking
◆ To link reading to mathematics and science

What to do

◆ Start by asking children to wash their hands and put on an apron.
◆ Give each child a copy of the recipe sheet and read through it with them.
◆ Explain to the children that they are going to make the cakes by following the recipe one step at a time.
◆ Give each child a bowl and spoon and help them go through the recipe.
◆ Explain to the children that the pictures will help them to understand what they have to do at each step.
◆ Finish by letting everyone enjoy the cakes.

Extension activities

◆ Try other simple recipes.
◆ Make a class recipe book.
◆ Invite the children to make up a magic recipe, for example a recipe for sweets that make you invisible.
◆ Follow sets of instructions for other activities. Look at instruction manuals.
◆ Look at other pieces of writing that provide information: posters, bus/train timetables, menus, dress patterns, etc.

Link to early learning goals
◆ Know that print carries meaning and, in English, is read from left to right and top to bottom

Chocolate rice snaps cakes recipe

Ingredients

2 chocolate bars
box of rice snaps cereal
cup
teaspoon

Equipment

mixing spoon
bowl
paper cake cases
fridge

What to do

Melt the chocolate. Let it cool.
Give each child a bowl and a mixing spoon.

1 Pour the chocolate into the bowls.

2 Measure one cup of rice snaps cereal.

3 Add the rice snaps to the chocolate.

4 Stir until well mixed.

5 Spoon the mixture into the paper cases.

6 Place the cakes in the fridge to set.

This page may be photocopied by the purchasing institution only.

Play Activities for the Early Years
www.brilliantpublications.co.uk

I am Goldilocks / Baby Bear

You will need
Book: *Goldilocks and the Three Bears*; Goldilocks mask (see page 54); Baby Bear mask (see page 55). Photocopy masks onto card and attach to lolly sticks.

What will the children learn?
◆ To understand the structure of a story
◆ To retell a story from a different perspective
◆ To act in character
◆ To express themselves and talk about emotions

Group size
Large groups

What to do
◆ Begin by reading the story *Goldilocks and the Three Bears.*
◆ Discuss how Goldilocks must have felt. How do you think she felt when she entered the house? How did she feel when she saw the three bears?
◆ Discuss how Baby Bear must have felt. Was he happy when walking in the forest? How do you think he felt when he saw his chair was broken?
◆ Show the children the masks.
◆ Now ask one child to put on the Goldilocks mask and tell the story as Goldilocks would have told it. For example, 'One day I was going for a walk in the woods when I saw a house. I went in the house and saw three bowls of porridge.'
◆ Now ask another child to put on the Baby Bear mask and tell the story as Baby Bear would. For example, 'One morning I woke up and Mum had made porridge for breakfast. It was too hot so Mum, Dad and I went for a walk.'
◆ The children might find this difficult to do so model the task for them to help give them ideas.
◆ Finish by leaving the masks in the dressing-up area for children to act out the story during free play.

Extension activities
◆ Make costumes to go with the masks.
◆ Retell the story from Mummy Bear's and Daddy Bear's perspective.
◆ Discuss how Goldilocks was wrong to go into a stranger's house. Talk about safety.
◆ Do the same activity for a different fairy tale, such as *The Three Little Pigs*. Make appropriate masks.
◆ Write stories from the perspective of different characters.

Link to early learning goals
◆ Show an understanding of the elements of stories, such as main characters, sequence of events and opening

Goldilocks mask

 Play Activities for the Early Years
www.brilliantpublications.co.uk

Baby Bear mask

Book about me

You will need

Scrap book; photos of children with their families (provided by children); pencils; felt-tip pens

Group size

Large groups

What will the children learn?
- To understand that information can be found in books
- To form a positive image of themselves
- To attempt to write simple sentences

What to do

- Explain to children that they are going to make an information book about themselves.
- Point out that books that provide information are called non-fiction books.
- Give each child a scrap book and ask them to bring in some photos of themselves and their families.
- Ask them to write simple sentences using words they know. Encourage them to attempt to write any words they do not know by using letter sounds.
- Allow them to work as independently as possible.
- Act as a scribe for children who are less confident.
- Finish by letting the children swap books with each other so they can learn about each other.
- Put the books in the book corner.

Extension activities

- Ask children to make a book about their best friend. They must first interview their friend to get the information they need.
- Read a variety of non-fiction books and point out the contents and index pages.
- Invite the children to use a computer to type up their work.
- Give children a pile of books and ask them to sort them into fiction and non-fiction.
- Ask children to sight read some words. Cover up the words and ask the children to try to write the words using their memory and knowledge of phonics.

Links to early learning goals
- Understand how information can be found in non-fiction texts to answer questions about where, who, why and how
- Use their phonic knowledge to write simple regular words and make phonetically plausible attempts at more complex words

Shopping at the supermarket

You will need

Labels for supermarket home corner (see pages 58 and 113); home corner set up as a supermarket with till, grocery items (tins, cereal packets, plastic fruit and vegetables, bottles), baskets and/or play shopping trolley

What will the children learn?
◆ To recognize that print carries meaning
◆ To write lists
◆ Role play
◆ To associate reading with everyday tasks

Group size

Small groups

What to do
◆ Set up the home corner as a supermarket.
◆ Before letting the children play in the home corner, place some grocery items on a table.
◆ Ask the children to make a list of the things they would like to buy from the supermarket.
◆ Encourage the children to use the packaging to find the words they need.
◆ Now place the items in the supermarket home corner.
◆ Invite the children to read their list and shop in the supermarket.
◆ Give each child a basket or trolley and play money.
◆ An adult should sit at the till to check the children have bought all the things on their list.

Extension activities
◆ Make a trip to a supermarket.
◆ Explore what other information can be found on food packaging.
◆ Ask children to sort some shopping into hoops, for example by colour, shape or size.
◆ Find out which countries different items come from.
◆ Talk about the names of different shopkeepers: baker, pharmacist, butcher, etc.
◆ The children could make their own packaging for some items.
◆ Design and make a till to use in the home corner (see Supermarket till, pages 112–113).

Links to early learning goals
◆ Know that print carries meaning
◆ Attempt writing for various purposes, using features of different forms such as lists, stories and instructions

Labels for supermarket home corner

customer	shopkeeper
manager	groceries
fruit and vegetables	dairy
bakery	frozen foods
till	money
receipt	shopping list
purse	trolley

Play Activities for the Early Years
www.brilliantpublications.co.uk

Mother's/Father's Day card

You will need
Card; felt-tip pens; photo of mother or father; decorative items; Mother's/Father's Day card words (see page 60); Patterns sheet (see page 61)

Group size
Large groups

What will the children learn?
◆ Card-making
◆ Pencil control – making simple patterns
◆ To read and write simple words
◆ Appreciation of their family
◆ To use letter sounds when reading and writing

What to do
◆ Talk to the children about Mother's/Father's Day and why we celebrate such days.
◆ Invite the children to make a card for their mother/father.
◆ Give each child a card and a copy of the Mother's/Father's Day card words sheet.
◆ Ask them to glue their parent's photo on the front of the card and to write 'My Mum' or 'My Dad' (using the words on the sheet to help them).
◆ Now show children the Pattern sheet and ask them to copy one of the patterns around their parent's photo to form a frame.
◆ Inside the card ask the children to use the sheet to help them write 'To Mum/Dad, I love you, from (name).'
◆ You may need to scribe for younger children.
◆ Show them how to use the sounds of letters (phonemes) to find the words they need.
◆ The children can take the finished cards home to give to their mother/father.

Extension activities
◆ Use different materials to make cards, for example dried flowers, different fabrics, collage materials.
◆ Make cards for different purposes: birthdays, best friend, thank you, etc.
◆ Use a software package on the computer to make cards.
◆ Make envelopes to go with the cards.
◆ Use the patterns on the Patterns sheet to decorate different items: name labels, picture frames, etc.

Links to early learning goals
◆ Attempt writing for various purposes, using features of different forms such as lists, stories and instructions
◆ Write their own names
◆ Use their phonic knowledge to write simple regular words
◆ Use a pencil and hold it effectively to form recognizable letters, most of which are correctly formed

Mother's/Father's Day card words

Happy Mother's Day	
Happy Father's Day	
to	Mum
Dad	I
love	you
from	with

This page may be photocopied by the purchasing institution only.

Play Activities for the Early Years
www.brilliantpublications.co.uk

Patterns sheet

Name t-shirt

You will need

Plain t-shirt; non-toxic fabric pens; newspaper; masking tape; Patterns sheet (see page 61)

Group size

Small groups

Patterns sheet (see page 61)

What will the children learn?

◆ To write their name
◆ To use a different medium – fabric pens
◆ Fine motor skills – finger–thumb grip for holding pens
◆ Letter formation

What to do

◆ Explain to children that they are going to design a t-shirt with their name on it.
◆ Lay the t-shirt flat on the table.
◆ Place a sheet of newspaper into the t-shirt to stop colour going through to the other side.
◆ To make it easier to write upon, fasten the t-shirt to the table using masking tape.
◆ Now ask children to write their name in the middle using the fabric pens. They can add patterns for decoration. The Patterns sheet provides some examples.
◆ Ensure the children are holding the pens correctly with a 'tripod' grip.
◆ Wash the t-shirts in a washing machine to set the colours.
◆ Let the children wear their t-shirts when they are dry.

Extension activities

◆ Use different themes, for example my family, my pet, my favourite animal, holidays, my school.
◆ Use the Patterns sheet to decorate different items such as cards or frames.
◆ Design other pieces of clothing such as trousers, jackets, hats.
◆ Practise writing names on different items, for example door labels, coat peg labels, exercise books.
◆ Try writing with different tools, for example cotton buds, feathers, paint brushes.

Links to early learning goals

◆ Write their own names
◆ Use a pencil and hold it effectively to form recognizable letters, most of which are correctly formed

Diary

You will need
Flip chart and pen; exercise books; pencils

Group size
Whole class

What will the children learn?
◆ Listening and speaking skills – in class discussion
◆ Independent writing
◆ To use phonics in reading and writing
◆ To begin to understand and use punctuation

What to do
◆ Try to do this activity every Monday morning.
◆ Sit children in a circle and discuss with them how they spent their weekend.
◆ Whilst they talk write some of their sentences on a flip chart, using punctuation.
◆ Give each child a diary book.
◆ Invite the children to draw a picture and write one sentence about their weekend in their diary book.
◆ Act as a scribe where necessary.
◆ Encourage them to write words they know and also to use their knowledge of letter sounds to try to write more complex words.
◆ Remind children to use punctuation – capital letter at the beginning and a full stop at the end.
◆ Finish with some children reading out their work.

Extension activities
◆ Invite some children to type their sentences on a computer.
◆ Pair up children and ask them to write about each other's weekend rather than their own.
◆ Have a display of common words to help children in their writing.
◆ Ask children to make up an imaginary story about their weekend. For example, 'I went on a flying carpet and went to Disneyland.' Record the stories on tape or scribe for the children.
◆ Write a sentence for each day of the week. For example, 'On Monday I played football. On Tuesday I wrote a story. On Wednesday….'
◆ Learn the days of the week.

Links to early learning goals
◆ Begin to form simple sentences, sometimes using punctuation
◆ Use their phonic knowledge to write simple regular words and make phonetically plausible attempts at more complex words

Three-letter words

You will need

Empty yoghurt pots; Three-letter words sheet (see page 65); glue; scissors; workbooks (or paper); pencils; flip chart and pen

Group size

Small groups

What to do

◆ Photocopy the sheet. Cut out the pictures on the sheet and stick them onto the pots. Cut out the letters and place them in the pots.
◆ Give one pot to each child.
◆ Ask the children to look at the picture on their pot and say what it is.
◆ Now ask them to take the letters out of the pot and put them in the right order to spell the word that matches the picture, for example p-e-n for 'pen'.
◆ Help the children by explaining that they must try to say the word slowly and think of the sounds.
◆ When they think they have the correct order ask them to write the word in their workbook (or on a sheet of paper).
◆ When the children have finished ask them to swap their pot with someone else and to try another word. Carry on until each child has had all the pots.
◆ At the end go through all the words and write them on the flip chart.

Extension activities

◆ Try the same activity with more complex words.
◆ Ask more able children to play this game verbally. For example, 'What word can you spell with the letters c, a, r?'
◆ Invite children to make words using wooden or plastic letters.
◆ Make greeting cards and encourage children to try to write simple messages (see Mother's/ Father's Day card, pages 59–60).
◆ Write sentences with missing words. Ask the children to try to fill in the missing word using phonics to work out the letters (see Finish the sentence, page 32).

Link to early learning goals

◆ Use their phonic knowledge to write simple regular words and make phonetically plausible attempts at more complex words

Three-letter words sheet

	s	u	n
	p	e	n
	c	a	t
	p	i	g
	c	a	r
	e	g	g

Chopstick challenge

You will need

Chopsticks or tweezers; small objects (buttons, beads, erasers, small world toys); pots; sand timer

Group size

Small groups

What will the children learn?
◆ The correct way to hold a pencil
◆ Hand–eye coordination
◆ Concentration
◆ Counting skills

What to do

◆ Lay out some small objects on a flat surface.
◆ Give each child a small pot and some chopsticks or tweezers.
◆ Show children how to use the chopsticks using a tripod grip.
◆ Explain to children that you are going to give them a challenge. The challenge is to pick up as many items as they can using the chopsticks before the sand timer finishes.
◆ Start the sand timer. Help the children to hold the chopsticks correctly.
◆ Count how many items each child has collected.

Extension activities

◆ Cook some noodles and ask children to try to eat them using the chopsticks.
◆ Put glue onto a picture and then sprinkle on some glitter or sand using a finger–thumb grip.
◆ Thread beads onto laces.
◆ Draw pictures or patterns using different tools, such as chalk, cotton buds, feathers.

Link to early learning goals
◆ Use a pencil and hold it effectively to form recognizable letters, most of which are correctly formed

Mathematical Development

In the early years, mathematics needs to be practical and fun. Young children need to encounter mathematical concepts in their daily lives and in practical situations, which are meaningful to the children themselves. It is also vitally important that children enjoy using numbers and this can be achieved in a variety of ways including games, stories, songs and play activities.

Mathematics can be broken down into four main areas: number, space, shape and measurement. Within these areas children need to develop a number of skills including matching, sorting, counting, investigating patterns, making links and looking at relationships.

The aim of this chapter is to help early years practitioners:

◆ help children build a strong foundation for future mathematical learning
◆ present mathematical concepts in a practical and fun way
◆ help children become confident at using numbers
◆ give children opportunities to use and talk about numbers in practical contexts
◆ enable children to experience the properties of shapes
◆ help children develop a positive attitude to mathematics.

The early learning goal of Mathematical Development is broken down into 11 learning opportunities, which are listed on the chart on page 68. Each learning opportunity is covered by at least three activities that will help children to achieve that target. The last column on the chart is for comments, and can be used for planning and assessment purposes.

Learning opportunities chart

Learning opportunity	Activities (and page numbers)	Comments
Say and use number names in order in familiar contexts	Number carpet tiles (69–70); Sand numbers (71); Garden hoop count (72)	
Count reliably up to 10 everyday objects	Sand numbers (71); Garden hoop count (72); Shape pizza (73); Sorting the laundry (74); Teddy bears' picnic (81); Speckled frogs book (82–83); Skittle game (87)	
Recognize numerals 1 to 9	Number carpet tiles (69–70); Sand numbers (71); Message in a bottle (75–76); Speckled frogs book (82–83); More/less game (84–85)	
Use language such as 'more' or 'less', 'greater' or 'smaller', 'heavier' or 'lighter' to compare two numbers or quantities	Planting bulbs (77); Garden hoop count (72); My foot (78)	
In practical activities and discussion begin to use the vocabulary involved in adding and subtracting	Garden hoop count (72); Ten little monkeys (79–80); Teddy bears' picnic (81)	
Find one more or one less than a number from 1 to 10	Speckled frogs book (82–83); More/less game (84–85); Tidy up toys (86)	
Begin to relate addition to combining two groups of objects, and subtraction to taking away	Teddy bears' picnic (81); Skittle game (87); Cuddly toys in bed (88–89)	
Talk about, recognize and recreate simple patterns	Sorting the laundry (74); Fruit kebabs (90); Butterfly pictures (91–92)	
Use language such as 'circle' or 'bigger' to describe the shape and size of solids and flat shapes	Shape pizza (73); Message in a bottle (75–76); Fruit kebabs (90); Cereal boxes (93)	
Use everyday words to describe position	Toy city (94); Robot game (95); Obstacle course (96)	
Use developing mathematical ideas and methods to solve practical problems	Sorting the laundry (74); Planting bulbs (77); The three bears (97)	

Number carpet tiles

You will need
Paints; paint brushes; 10 plain carpet tiles; Number cards (see page 70)

Group size
Small groups

What will the children learn?
◆ To recognize numbers 1–10
◆ Matching and sorting skills – reasoning and decision-making – the same essential skills needed when learning to read

What to do
◆ Paint numbers 1–10 onto the tiles using brightly coloured paints to attract and interest the children. Leave to dry.
◆ In a large room (or even outside) lay the tiles in a line, starting with 1 and finishing with 10. Ask the children to help you.
◆ Explain to the children that you would like them to jump from one number to the next, shouting out the numbers as they go.
◆ Make the jumping fun as children learn more when they are enjoying themselves.
◆ Now give each child a number card and ask them to place it on the matching number tile.
◆ Praise the children for each attempt.
◆ Finish the activity by collecting the tiles, counting backwards from 10 to 1.

Extension activities
◆ This game can be developed further. For example, you could do counting on, counting back, counting in twos, fives, etc.
◆ Ask children to put the correct number of objects onto each carpet tile, for example five pencils on number 5.
◆ Play musical numbers. When the music stops the children have to jump onto a number – remove one tile and play the music again.
◆ Use the tiles for number songs and rhymes such as 'Ten Green Bottles', 'Ten Little Monkeys Jumping on the Bed', 'Ten Fat Sausages', 'Ten Currant Buns' (see Ten little monkeys, pages 79–80, and Speckled frogs book, (pages 82–83).
◆ Extend the activity by adding actions, such as hopping. When the child reaches the number 4 tile they have to hop four times.

Links to early learning goals
◆ Say and use number names in order
◆ Recognize numerals 1 to 9

Number cards

1	6
2	7
3	8
4	9
5	10

 Play Activities for the Early Years
www.brilliantpublications.co.uk

Sand numbers

You will need
Large pieces of card (eg A5 size); glue; pencils; sand

Group size
Small groups

What will the children learn?
◆ Number names and number-writing
◆ Ordering and counting skills
◆ To develop their tactile ability
◆ Correct finger grip

What to do
◆ Begin by explaining to the children that they are going to make some number cards.
◆ Write the numbers 1–10 on the cards.
◆ Ask the children to squeeze or paint glue onto the numbers and then sprinkle with the sand. You can add food colouring to the sand to make it more colourful.
◆ Once the cards are finished and dry, encourage the children to trace over the numbers with their fingers while you say what each one is. For example, 'This is number one.'
◆ Ensure the children trace the numbers in the same direction they would normally write them.

Extension activities
◆ Instead of sand you could use rice or cereal – anything with a texture (see Textured pictures, page 134).
◆ On the reverse side stick pictures of the appropriate number of objects. For exmple, for number 1 stick one bike, for number 2 stick two balls, etc.
◆ Encourage the children to look at the pictures so that they begin to relate the numerals to the quantities they represent. Using pictures of everyday objects provides a link between solid objects and mathematics.
◆ Ask the children to put the cards in the correct order from 1 to 10.
◆ Have a bowl of counters and ask the children to put the right number of counters on each card.
◆ Make another set of cards and play a game of Snap.
◆ Make some sand pictures (see Sand pictures, page 135).
◆ Blindfold a child and ask them to try to identify plastic numbers just by feeling their shape.

Links to early learning goals
◆ Say and use number names in order
◆ Count reliably up to 10 everyday objects
◆ Recognize numerals 1 to 9

Garden hoop count

You will need
Hoops; paper; pens

Group size
Small groups

What to do

- First give each child a hoop and ask them to place it anywhere in the school garden.
- Then ask them to guess how many leaves, flowers, ants, etc they think they will find in the hoop.
- Record their guesses on a pictorial chart.
- Once they have guessed ask them to count how many there actually are. Record their findings on the chart.
- Ask the children to see if the number they guessed was more or less than the actual number, and by how many.
- Now do the same again but in a different part of the garden.

What will the children learn?
- Awareness of their environment – looking for similarities and differences
- Counting and addition skills
- To understand and use the terms 'more' and 'less'
- To record their findings in a chart
- Observational skills

Extension activities

- You can count a variety of things: stones, leaves, twigs, berries, beetles, etc.
- Talk about the results they found in different parts of the garden. For example, 'Why were there more flowers in one part than in another?'
- Show different ways of presenting results, for example bar charts, pie charts.
- Do the same activity but in a different location, such as the seaside, park or town centre (see Trip to the park, page 122).
- Collect some items to use when making nature collages or mobiles (see Seaside collage, page 123, and Park collage, page 133).
- Find out more about the minibeasts the children find (see Minibeast safari, page 153).
- Write a list of all the things they find.
- Discuss how the children can look after their local environment.

Links to early learning goals
- Say and use number names in order in familiar contexts
- Count reliably up to 10 everyday objects
- Use language such as 'more' or' less'
- In practical activities and discussion begin to use the vocabulary involved in adding

Shape pizza

You will need

1 pizza base; tomato puree;
3 rectangular pieces of ham; 4
circular pieces of tomato;
5 triangular pieces of cheese; 6
spherical olives; 7 triangular
pieces of pineapple; 8 pieces of
sweetcorn; baking tray; large
plate; oven; knife

What will the children learn?

◆ To identify and name different shapes – both flat and
  solid
◆ Counting skills
◆ Cooking provides a practical way of combining
  maths and science

Group size

Small groups

What to do

◆ Begin by explaining to the children that they are going to make a pizza.
◆ Place the pizza base on a baking tray. Talk about the shape.
◆ Squeeze two oval squirts of tomato puree onto the base and ask, 'What shape is this?'
◆ Ask one child to spread the puree all over the base.
◆ Place the ingredients on a large plate and talk to the children about the different shapes. For
  example, 'What shape are the tomato slices?'
◆ Arrange the ingredients on the pizza, counting out the quantities.
◆ Bake in an oven at 220°C/425°F/gas mark 7 for 10 minutes. Cut up and enjoy.

Extension activities

◆ Encourage the children to not only look at the shapes but also feel them (using more than one
  sense enhances learning).
◆ Use a cardboard base and paper toppings to make an imaginary pizza.
◆ When cutting the pizza talk about halves and quarters.
◆ Make a salad and garlic bread to go with the pizza.
◆ Talk about healthy/unhealthy food (see Healthy food plate, page 164).
◆ Make a bar chart of the children's favourite pizza toppings.
◆ Write a shopping list of the ingredients.

Links to early learning goals

◆ Count reliably up to 10 everyday objects
◆ Use language such as 'circle' to describe the shape of solids and flat shapes

Sorting the laundry

You will need
Variety of newly washed laundry: socks, tops, trousers, dresses, etc

Group size
Whole class, then small groups

What will the children learn?
◆ To understand the link between mathematics and everyday activities
◆ Sorting and matching skills
◆ To count 10 everyday objects
◆ To recognize and name colours

What to do
◆ Start by talking about laundry and how clothes are washed and then dried. Relate it to their own lives. Who does the laundry at home? How is it sorted and put away?
◆ Lay out the clothes and ask children how they could sort it out.
◆ Different ways of sorting could include:
  ❖ adult clothes, children's clothes
  ❖ by colour
  ❖ by item: all socks, all trousers, etc.
◆ Finally ask them which is the best way to sort out the laundry.

Extension activities
◆ This activity could be used on different occasions:
  ❖ lunchtime – sort out the cutlery
  ❖ tidying up toys
  ❖ putting away the groceries.
◆ Count out the numbers of each type of clothing: 'How many socks are there?'
◆ Wash and dry some doll's clothes. Talk about how the clothes are washed and dried. Discuss how the water and soap clean the clothes and the sun and wind dry them.
◆ Encourage them to make comparisons between wet and dry clothes.
◆ Look at the different textures of the clothes and also the different patterns they can see (see Patterned jumper, pages 107–108).
◆ Read *Doing the Washing* by Sarah Garland (Puffin Playschool Books).

Links to early learning goals
◆ Count reliably up to 10 everyday objects
◆ Talk about and recognize simple patterns
◆ Use developing mathematical ideas and methods to solve practical problems

Message in a bottle

You will need
Different size bottles with lids; paddling pool; Messages sheet (see page 76); garden sticks; string; magnets and magnetic tape

What will the children learn?
◆ Observational skills
◆ To recognize and write numbers
◆ Introduction to magnets and their properties
◆ To identify and observe features in the natural world
◆ Hand–eye coordination and pre-writing skills

Group size
Small groups

What to do
◆ Begin by explaining to the children that they are going to make a game and then play it.
◆ Show children the 'outside' messages and ask them to put a different one in each bottle. Put the lids on the bottles.
◆ Now ask the children to paint a number (1–10) on each bottle.
◆ On the lid of each bottle put a small strip of magnetic tape.
◆ Invite children to make fishing rods by tying a magnet to a string and then attaching it to a garden stick.
◆ Fill up a paddling pool with water.
◆ Place the sealed bottles into the pool.
◆ Give each child a fishing rod and let them go fishing.
◆ When a child catches a bottle ask them what number it is.
◆ Help the child to read the message inside the bottle. Then let them do the task given in the message.

Extension activities
◆ Other messages could ask children to find the biggest/smallest tree, plant, stone, bush, ball, leaf, toy, chair, etc.
◆ Extend activity by introducing terms such as 'big', 'bigger', 'biggest' and 'small', 'smaller', 'smallest'.
◆ This game can be adapted so it can be played indoors. Instead of the paddling pool you could fill the sink with water. See the Messages sheet for possible messages.
◆ Talk to the children about how the magnets stick to the bottles and let them find other things in the classroom that the magnets stick to.
◆ Decorate the bottles as boats.
◆ Discuss floating and sinking, and investigate.
◆ This activity would be a great party game.

Links to early learning goals
◆ Recognize numerals 1 to 9
◆ Use language such as 'bigger'/'smaller' to describe the size of solids and flat shapes

Messages sheet

Outside

Find the biggest flower and the smallest flower.
Find the biggest tree and the smallest tree.
Find the biggest stone and the smallest stone.
Find the biggest bush and the smallest bush.
Find the biggest stick and the smallest stick.
Find the biggest seed and the smallest seed.
Find the biggest paving stone and the smallest paving stone.
Find the biggest leaf and the smallest leaf.
Find the biggest conker and the smallest conker.
Find the biggest feather and the smallest feather.

Inside

Find the biggest book and the smallest book.
Find the biggest toy car and the smallest toy car.
Find the biggest chair and the smallest chair.
Find the biggest teddy bear and the smallest teddy bear.
Find the biggest doll and the smallest doll.
Find the biggest pencil and the smallest pencil.
Find the biggest pot and the smallest pot.
Find the biggest jigsaw and the smallest jigsaw.
Find the biggest bottle and the smallest bottle.
Find the biggest paint brush and the smallest paint brush.

 Play Activities for the Early Years
www.brilliantpublications.co.uk

Planting bulbs

You will need
Variety of plant pots; variety of bulbs; bag of compost; trowel; small bucket

Group size
Small groups

What will the children learn?
◆ To use their mathematical knowledge to solve a practical problem
◆ To understand in practical terms the terms 'more'/ 'less', 'greater'/'smaller', 'heavier'/'lighter'
◆ To estimate and verify results – an important part of both mathematics and science

What to do
◆ Explain to the children that they are going to plant some bulbs.
◆ Lay out the plant pots according to size, from the biggest to the smallest.
◆ Ask the children to guess how many buckets would be needed to fill each pot.
◆ Record the guesses and then fill each one and see if the guesses were correct. Discuss which pot needed the most and which needed the least.
◆ Compare which pot is the heaviest and which is the lightest.
◆ Have a look at the bulbs and compare. Place them in order of size and then in order of weight (heaviest to lightest).
◆ Plant the bulbs in the pots, water them, then place them on the windowsill.
◆ Water regularly and let children observe how the plants grow.

Extension activities
◆ Ask questions whilst doing the activity to get the children thinking: 'Which pot will hold the most compost? Which pot will hold the biggest number of bulbs? Is the pot heavier with or without compost? Which bulb is heavier/ lighter?'
◆ Ask the children to guess which bulb will grow to be the tallest plant. Label the pots with the children's guesses. Then record the growth over a number of weeks and see whose guess was correct.
◆ Discuss how the bulbs need water, compost and light in order to grow (see My own garden, page 104).
◆ Plant bulbs in different conditions. For example, you could grow one without water, one in the dark, etc.
◆ Discuss the similarities and differences between the plants grown.
◆ Name the parts of a plant.

Links to early learning goals
◆ Use language such as 'more' or 'less', 'greater' or 'smaller', 'heavier' or 'lighter' to compare quantities
◆ Use developing mathematical ideas and methods to solve practical problems

My foot

You will need

Paper; pencils; scissors; child's shoe; classroom items

Group size

Small groups

What will the children learn?

- ◆ To order items by length
- ◆ To understand in practical terms 'longer' and 'shorter'
- ◆ To use their body for measurement
- ◆ Fine motor skills – drawing and cutting

What to do

- ◆ Discuss the terms 'longer' and 'shorter'. Show and talk about different items. For example, 'This pencil is shorter than this pencil.'
- ◆ Ask children to draw around their foot and cut it out.
- ◆ Now ask the children to look around the classroom for three items which are shorter than their foot.
- ◆ Then ask them to look for three items longer than their foot.
- ◆ Ask children to compare their foot cut-out to another child's. Is it longer or shorter?
- ◆ Finish by asking the children to put their foot cut-outs in a row from the shortest to the longest.

Extension activities

- ◆ Instead of a drawing round their foot children could draw round their hand.
- ◆ Do some feet or hand printing. Cut out the print and use it for measuring.
- ◆ Ask children to find items of different lengths in the classroom.
- ◆ Measure the children's height. Who is the tallest? Who is the shortest?
- ◆ Look at Mehndi patterns on feet and hands.

Link to early learning goals

- ◆ Use language such as 'greater' or 'smaller', 'heavier' or 'lighter' to compare quantities

Ten little monkeys

You will need

Monkey sheet (see page 80); garden sticks; sticky tape; scissors; felt-tip pens; bed sheet; table

Group size

Large group

What will the children learn?
◆ To understand and use the vocabulary for addition and subtraction
◆ To recite and memorize a song – songs are an entertaining way to learn about numbers
◆ Fine motor skills – cutting and gluing
◆ Creativity and imagination

What to do
◆ Give the children a copy of the Monkey sheet each and ask them to cut out the monkey and colour it in.
◆ Attach a garden stick to the back of the cut-out using sticky tape.
◆ Place a bed sheet on a table to represent the monkeys' bed.
◆ Ask the children to kneel behind the table and move the monkeys up and down so that the monkeys look like they are jumping on the bed.
◆ Now ask the children to sing the song 'Ten Little Monkeys Jumping on the Bed' (see the Monkey sheet for the words).
◆ After each verse ask one child to remove their monkey.
◆ Ask the children questions: How many monkeys were on the bed? How many monkeys jumped off? How many monkeys are left?
◆ Carry on until there are no more monkeys left.

Extension activities
◆ Write numbers (1–10) on the monkeys.
◆ For younger children, only use five monkeys.
◆ For older children, adapt the song so that, instead of jumping off individually, they jump off in pairs.
◆ Attach an elastic string to the monkey cut-outs so they can be bounced up and down.
◆ In a PE lesson ask the children to pretend they are monkeys jumping on the bed. Use a trampoline or crash mat as a bed. Ask the children to act out the song.
◆ Use the monkeys for counting activities.
◆ Instead of monkeys use other items, such as frogs (see Speckled frogs book, pages 82–83).

Link to early learning goals
◆ In practical activities and discussion begin to use the vocabulary involved in adding and subtracting

Monkey sheet

Ten Little Monkeys

Ten little monkeys jumping on the bed
One fell off and bumped his head.
Mummy called the doctor and the doctor said,
'No more monkeys jumping on the bed.'

Nine little monkeys jumping on the bed
One fell off and bumped his head.
Mummy called the doctor and the doctor said,
'No more monkeys jumping on the bed.'

Eight little monkeys jumping on the bed…

 Play Activities for the Early Years
www.brilliantpublications.co.uk

Teddy bears' picnic

You will need
5 cuddly teddy bears; tea set; food; picnic blanket

Group size
Small groups

What to do
◆ Lay out the blanket and explain to the children that they are going to have a picnic with their teddy bears.
◆ Count out the teddies and place them around the blanket.
◆ Now count out some plates (ensure you start by only giving four).
◆ Give them out and ask:
  ❖ Are there enough plates?
  ❖ Do we need any more?
  ❖ How many more do we need?
◆ Now hand out the cups (start with only seven cups).
◆ Give them out and ask:
  ❖ Have we got enough cups?
  ❖ How many do we need?
  ❖ How many shall we take away?
◆ Do similar tasks with the knives and forks.
◆ When everything is laid out, give out the food and enjoy the picnic.

What will the children learn?
◆ To count from 1 to 10
◆ To use and understand the terms 'more' and 'less'
◆ To use addition and subtraction in an everyday situation
◆ To think visually
◆ To understand that subtraction involves taking away and addition involves the combination of two quantities
◆ Creativity, imagination and fun in mathematics

Extension activities
◆ A similar activity can be done at lunchtime when laying the table.
◆ The teddies can be used for other mathematical activities. For example, 'Which teddy is the tallest/oldest?'
◆ Sort the teddies into hoops by size, colour, etc.
◆ Ask the children to make a list of food for the picnic.
◆ Cook some food for the picnic: biscuits, cakes, sandwiches, etc (see Alphabet biscuits, pages 42–43, Chocolate rice snaps, pages 51–52).
◆ Make up stories for the teddies.

Links to early learning goals
◆ Count reliably up to 10 everyday objects
◆ In practical activities and discussion begin to use the vocabulary involved in adding and subtracting
◆ Begin to relate addition to combining two groups of objects, and subtraction to taking away

Speckled frogs book

You will need

Empty photo album (with peel-back plastic sheets); frogs cut from Speckled frogs sheet (see page 83) – each child will need at least 15 frogs; glue; pencil

Group size

Small groups

What will the children learn?

◆ Counting skills
◆ To recognize numerals and practise number-writing
◆ To understand and use the terms 'one less' and 'one more'
◆ To develop memory skills by singing a repetitive song

What to do

◆ Sing the song 'Five Little Speckled Frogs' with the children (see Speckled frogs sheet for words).
◆ Discuss as a group how they are going to make a book to go with the song.
◆ Open the album and peel open the plastic sheet.
◆ Give each child a pile of frogs.
◆ Ask children to count out five frogs and stick them into the album.
◆ Write the numeral 5 underneath and seal the page.
◆ Next ask: 'If one frog jumps away how many will be left?' Use the frogs to help visualization.
◆ Use the terms 'take away' and 'one less'.
◆ Count out four frogs and stick them on the next page. Write the numeral 4 underneath.
◆ Carry on with this process until you get to zero.
◆ Finish the activity by singing the song again whilst looking at the book.

Extension activities

◆ By using a photo album with clear plastic you can use the book for number practice. The children can write over the numbers with a non-permanent felt-tip pen and then wipe clean to use again.
◆ Do the book in reverse to show the children how many is one more than a number (see Ten little monkeys, pages 79–80, and Cuddly toys in bed, page 88).
◆ Do the same activity but with different songs. Possibilities include: 'Ten Green Bottles Sitting on a Wall', 'Ten in a Bed', 'Five Currant Buns in the Baker's Shop' and 'Five Fat Sausages'.
◆ Act out the song with the children pretending to be frogs.
◆ Look at the life cycle of frogs. If the school has a pond let children observe frogs as they develop.
◆ Make frogs by using a variety of art resources: clay, papier mâché, etc.
◆ Write a whole-class story about a frog.

Links to early learning goals

◆ Count reliably up to 10 everyday objects
◆ Recognize numerals 1 to 9
◆ Find one more or one less than a number from 1 to 10

Speckled frogs sheet

Five Little Speckled Frogs

Five little speckled frogs
Sat on a speckled log,
Eating some most delicious bugs,
Yum, yum.
One jumped into the pool,
Where it was nice and cool,
Now there are four speckled frogs,
Glug, glug.

Four little speckled frogs…

More/less game

You will need

Number cards sheet (see page 70) photocopied onto blue, red and green card and cut up to make three sets of cards; More/less dice sheet (see page 85) photocopied onto card to make a more/less dice; glue

What will the children learn?

◆ Social skills such as cooperation and listening
◆ Counting skills and number recognition
◆ To understand and use the terms 'one more' and 'one less'
◆ To interpret the meaning of numbers; to think about the significance of what they mean

Group size

Pairs

What to do

◆ Explain to children that they are going to play a card game. Ask the children to work in pairs.
◆ Lay out the red set of number cards face up on the table.
◆ Give the blue set of cards to child **A** and the green set of cards to child **B**. Both sets need to be in piles face down.
◆ Ask child **A** to turn over their top card and read the number.
◆ Next ask them to throw the dice.
◆ If they get the side '1 more' explain that they have to choose a number from the red set which is 1 more than the number on their card. So, if they got 4 they need to pick number 5 from the red pack.
◆ Now put those cards to the side.
◆ Next it is child **B**'s turn to do the same.
◆ As the number of red cards decreases there will be occasions when a card cannot be picked as it has already gone.
◆ The game ends when all the red cards have gone.
◆ The winner is the one with the most red cards at the end.

Extension activities

◆ Change the quantity on the dice, for example '2 more' and '2 less'.
◆ Let the children use counters to help them find the numbers they need.
◆ Use the dice for other games.

Links to early learning goals

◆ Recognize numerals 1 to 9
◆ Find one more or one less than a number from 1 to 10

More/less dice sheet

1 more

1 less   1 less   1 more

1 more

1 less

Tidy up toys

You will need
A variety of small toys; toy box; flip chart and pen

Group size
Small groups

What to do
◆ Show the children the toy box and explain that you are going to hand out the toys one at a time.
◆ Start by giving each child one toy. Ask the children to count how many toys they have.
◆ Now give each child another toy and ask the children how many toys they have now.
◆ Write on the flip chart, 'Two is one more than one.' Read it aloud with the children.
◆ Underneath write, 'One add one is two.' Read aloud with the children again.
◆ Repeat the above until each child has ten toys.
◆ Allow the children time to play with their toys.
◆ Now explain to the children that it is tidy up time and that you need their help to put the toys back in the toy box.
◆ Ask the children to place their toys in a row and to count how many they have.
◆ Show the children the toy box and ask them to put one of their toys into it.
◆ Now ask them to count how many are left.
◆ Write on the flip chart, and ask children to read with you, 'Nine is one less than ten.'
◆ Underneath write, 'Ten take away one is nine.' Ask the children to read it with you.
◆ Repeat the above until all the toys are in the toy box. Thank the children for helping to tidy up.

Extension activities
◆ For younger children, use just five toys.
◆ For older children add and take away two toys at a time.
◆ Do the same activity with different resources such as balls and pots. Ask the children to place the balls in a pot one at a time using a spoon.
◆ Fasten number labels on the toys.
◆ In a PE lesson ask the children to stand together on a mat. Count how many children there are. Now ask the children to jump off the mat one at a time. Count how many children are left after each child has jumped.

Link to early learning goals
◆ Find one more or one less than a number from 1 to 10

Skittle game

You will need
10 empty plastic bottles (with lids); small ball; sand; counters

Group size
Small groups

What will the children learn?
◆ Counting skills
◆ To understand that addition involves the combination of two groups of objects
◆ Hand–eye coordination
◆ To coordinate bodily movements and improve balance
◆ Social skills – turn-taking and following a set of rules

What to do
◆ Explain to the children that they are going to make a skittles game. Explain that it is similar to ten-pin bowling.
◆ Start by asking the children to fill the bottles a third of the way up with sand so they are a little more stable. Put the lids on the bottles.
◆ Arrange the bottles in a triangular pattern as in a game of ten-pin bowling.
◆ Each person gets two turns to throw the ball. After each turn count the number of skittles that have fallen and give the child the equivalent number of counters.
◆ After both turns the player has to add up how many counters there are in total to find their score.
◆ The winner is the one that has knocked down the most skittles.

Extension activities
◆ Decorate the bottles using bright coloured paints.
◆ Record the results on a chart so that the children can keep a record of the game. This will give a pictorial representation of the addition that has taken place.
◆ Practise number bonds by working out how many skittles have been knocked down and how many are still standing.
◆ For more able children, put a number on each bottle and score by adding up the numbers knocked down with each throw.
◆ If you don't have plastic bottles you could use a bean bag and decorated toilet roll tubes.
◆ Make up different games using the bottles and ball.

Links to early learning goals
◆ Count reliably up to 10
◆ Begin to relate addition to combining two groups of objects

Cuddly toys in bed

You will need

10 cuddly toys, 2 cardboard boxes; 2 doll's blankets or pieces of fabric; Cuddly toys in bed sheet (see page 89). Photocopy the spinner onto card and cut out. Fasten pointer to spinner with split pin.

What will the children learn?
◆ Counting skills
◆ That subtraction means taking away
◆ To think visually about subtraction
◆ Role play and imagination
◆ Social skills – taking turns and following rules

Group size

Pairs

What to do

◆ Show the children the toys and explain that they are going to play a game with them.
◆ Make the boxes into beds and cover with the blankets.
◆ Count out the toys and put five in one box and five in other. Give each child a bed.
◆ The children take it in turns to spin the spinner.
◆ After each spin the child takes away the appropriate number of toys and counts how many are left.
◆ The winner is the one who has an empty bed first.

Extension activities

◆ For older children, increase the number of toys in each bed to ten.
◆ Write down the results after each spin to give a more pictorial representation of the subtraction that has taken place.
◆ Back up the game by singing 'Ten in the Bed' (see sheet for words).
◆ Order the toys from the smallest to the biggest.
◆ Ask the children to make the right size bed and cover for each toy.
◆ Sort the toys into hoops, for example or by colour or size.

Link to early learning goals
◆ Begin to relate subtraction to taking away

Cuddly toys in bed sheet

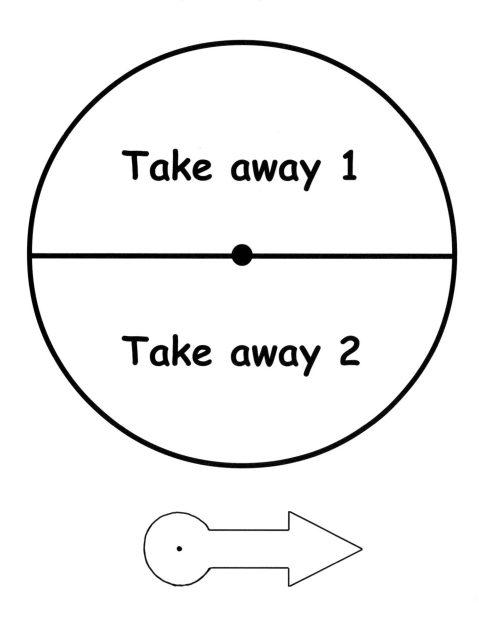

Ten in the Bed
There were ten in the the bed
And the little one said,
'Roll over, roll over.'
So they all rolled over
And one fell out
There were nine in the bed
And the little one said...

Continue until...
There was one in the bed
And the little one said,
'Thank goodness, peace at last.'

Fruit kebabs

You will need

Assorted fruit (seedless green grapes, red apples, oranges, melons, plums, etc); blunt knives; plates; dull-tipped kebab sticks

Group size

Small groups

What to do

◆ Explain to children that they are going to make some fruit kebabs.
◆ Start by naming each of the fruits and talk about how they look (colour, shape, etc).
◆ Cut the fruit into different shapes. Ask the children to help using blunt knives.
◆ When cutting the fruit use terms such as 'half' and 'quarter'.
◆ Show children how to make a simple repetitive pattern using the fruit, for example one banana, one orange.
◆ Now ask the children to form their own pattern with the fruit on a plate.
◆ Transfer this pattern onto the kebab sticks.
◆ Finish the activity by eating the resulting patterns.

Extension activities

◆ Instead of using a knife to cut up the fruit the children could use biscuit cutters.
◆ The children could record their pattern by drawing it on paper. For example, they could use an orange circle for an orange and a yellow circle for a banana.
◆ Make repetitive patterns using beads and strings.
◆ Use fruit for printing and make repetitive patterns.
◆ Blindfold one child and ask them to taste different fruits and guess what they are.
◆ Talk about how the snack is very healthy (see Healthy food plate, page 164).

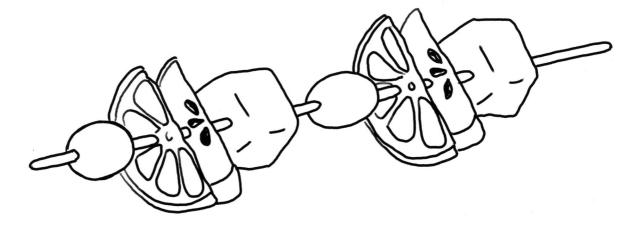

Links to early learning goals

◆ Recreate and record simple patterns
◆ Use language to describe the shape of solids and flat shapes

Play Activities for the Early Years
www.brilliantpublications.co.uk

Butterfly pictures

You will need
Butterfly cut-out sheet (see page 92); paints; hand lenses; pictures of butterflies; brushes

Group size
Whole class, then small groups

What will the children learn?
◆ Observational skills
◆ To recognize that patterns occur in nature
◆ To recreate patterns using paint
◆ Creativity but also appreciation of symmetry and balance

What to do
◆ Weather permitting, start by going for a walk in the garden/park to enable the children to see real butterflies. Use hand lenses to get a good look.
◆ Look at pictures of butterflies and talk about the patterns. Ask questions: What patterns can they see? Are both wings the same?
◆ Give each child a copy of the Butterfly cut-out sheet and explain that they are going to paint patterns on the wings.
◆ Fold the butterfly cut-out in half and then open up.
◆ Invite the children to paint a pattern on just one side.
◆ Fold the cut-out in half again and press down firmly.
◆ Open out the paper and discuss the pattern that has been made.
◆ Finish the activity by displaying the butterflies.
◆ You could attach string to the butterflies and hang them from the ceiling.

Extension activities
◆ Discuss the features of a butterfly: antennae, head, etc. When the paint is dry the children could add more features: feelers, body, etc.
◆ Find other patterns in nature.
◆ Ask children to design their own pattern.
◆ Make a pattern using beads and ask the children to copy it.
◆ Look at patterns in clothing (see Patterned jumper, pages 107–108).
◆ Talk about how butterflies are small and delicate and how the children can study them but must also be very careful with them.
◆ Explain the word 'symmetry' by looking at pictures of butterfly wings. Use mirrors to help the children understand.
◆ Read the book *The Very Hungry Caterpillar* by Eric Carle (Puffin Books). Find out about the life cycle of a butterfly (see The Very Hungry Caterpillar, page 139).

Link to early learning goals
◆ Talk about, recognize and recreate simple patterns

Butterfly cut-out sheet

 Play Activities for the Early Years
www.brilliantpublications.co.uk

Cereal boxes

You will need
A variety of empty cereal boxes; glue; small sticky paper shapes

Group size
Small groups

What to do
- Give each child an empty cereal box.
- Explain that you would like them to unfold the box so it is flat.
- Help children with the unfolding to ensure there is no tearing.
- Once the box is flat ask children to count how many 2D shapes they can see. How many rectangles? How many triangles? etc.
- Ask children to count how many 2D shapes the box is made up of.
- Introduce words such as 'face', 'corner', 'edge'.
- Now ask the children to fold and glue to make a box again.
- Finish by decorating the box with some sticky paper shapes. The box can be used for storing items.

What will the children learn?
- 2D and 3D shape names
- To understand that 3D shapes are made up of 2D shapes
- Mathematical terms to describe 3D shapes: 'faces', 'corners', etc
- Fine motor control – folding, unfolding, gluing

Extension activities
- Older children could glue the boxes inside out to give a blank surface to decorate.
- Show how a cube is made up of six squares.
- Unfold other 3D shapes, for example a pyramid.
- Use 3D boxes to make a robot (see Robot game, page 95).
- Do some printing using a variety of 3D shapes.
- Use 2D and 3D objects for PE, for example hoops, mats, tunnels and boxes (see Obstacle course, page 96, and Going on a bear hunt, page 165).

Link to early learning goals
- Use language such as 'circle' or 'bigger' to describe the shape and size of solids and flat shapes

Toy city

You will need

Variety of junk material (milk cartons, cereal boxes, egg boxes, bottles, and yoghurt pots); twigs; very large piece of cardboard; paint; paint brushes; paper; toy cars

Group size

Whole class, then small groups

What will the children learn?

- To use mathematical language to describe positions
- To work as a team and learn to interact and plan with others
- To listen, and appreciate the importance of understanding and following instructions
- Visual/spatial intelligence and creativity

What to do

- This is a big project that can be spread over a number of days.
- Explain to the children that they are going to make a city for their toys.
- Begin by planning with the children how they are going to make their toy city.
- From the plan and the material available work with them to make the toy city. The city can be made on a large sheet of cardboard so that it can be tidied away if necessary.
- When complete, let the children use the toy cars to drive around the city.
- Ask the children to give you directions to get from one part of the city to another. For example, how can you get from the hospital to the school? The children may tell you to go forward and then turn left and then go under the bridge.
- Let the children have fun exploring their city.

Extension activities

- Go for a walk in the local area. Point out key features such as the school, church, hospital, post box, etc (see Where we live, page 124).
- Use construction kits to make the toy city.
- Ask children how they get to school from their home. Record in writing for them.
- Play an opposites game. Ask: What is the opposite of forwards? What is the opposite of left? Play a game where every time you shout an instruction they have to do the opposite.
- Count how many items are in the toy city. How many houses? Cars? Roads?
- Make up a story about their toys in the toy city.
- Make a house for their favourite toy using junk material.

Link to early learning goals
- Use everyday words to describe position

Robot game

You will need

A variety of junk material (cardboard boxes, egg boxes, bottles, tubes, cereal boxes, etc); sticky tape; paint; scissors; a gift/treasure (eg chocolate or a toy)

Group size

Pairs

What will the children learn?

◆ To use mathematical language to describe positions (prepositions)
◆ To work together harmoniously
◆ Listening skills and the importance of understanding, following and giving instructions
◆ To imitate, act and be aware of their bodies

What to do

◆ Explain to the children that they are going to play a robot game.
◆ Divide the children into pairs: one child is the robot and the other is the instructor.
◆ Ask the children to use the material provided to dress up one child as a robot.
◆ The instructor should then hide some treasure in the classroom whilst the robot closes its eyes.
◆ The instructor now gives the robot instructions so that it can find the treasure.
◆ When giving instructions ask children to use words such as: 'move forward three steps', 'turn left', 'go under the table', etc.
◆ The activity ends when the robot finds the treasure. The children could then swap roles.

Extension activities

◆ Do a movement lesson and ask children to pretend they are a robot.
◆ Make up a story or poem about a robot.
◆ Ask children to think about what they would like a robot to do for them, for example clean up their room, or go shopping. Draw a picture of what it would look like.
◆ Count how many of each body part the robot has.

Link to early learning goals

◆ Use everyday words to describe position

Obstacle course

You will need
A map of the local area around the school; PE equipment set up as an obstacle course

Group size
Whole class, then small groups

What will the children learn?
◆ Gross motor skills – coordination and balance
◆ Creativity and imagination
◆ Opposites: over/under, up/down, etc
◆ To use mathematical language to describe positions (prepositions)

What to do
◆ Begin by looking at the map of the school and the local area.
◆ Mark the school and point out key areas, such as the post box, traffic lights, bridge, etc.
◆ Ask the children how they travel to school and the route they take.
◆ Ask them to describe their journey – 'walk across the road', 'turn left', 'go over the bridge', etc.
◆ Show the children the apparatus.
◆ Invite the children to find as many different ways of travelling over, under, through and around the apparatus.
◆ Encourage the children to describe what they are doing using words such as 'under', 'on', 'over', 'through'.
◆ Finish by choosing some children to demonstrate their work. Ask them to describe their actions as they do them.

Extension activities
◆ Rearrange the equipment and ask children to find different ways of travelling (see Going on a bear hunt, page 165).
◆ Older children may be able to set up their own obstacle course.
◆ Count how many different ways they can travel on a piece of apparatus.
◆ Make a bar chart of the different ways the children travel to school, for example walk, car, bicycle.
◆ Ask children to draw a map of their route to school.
◆ Invite the children to make up an imaginary journey, for example to a treasure island.

Link to early learning goals
◆ Use everyday words to describe position

The three bears

You will need

Book: *Goldilocks and the Three Bears*; brown card; pencils; scissors; garden sticks; sticky tape; doll

Group size

Whole class, then small groups

What will the children learn?

◆ To use their mathematical knowledge of size to solve a problem
◆ To order items by length
◆ Fine motor skills – cutting and gluing
◆ Listening and speaking skills – listening to a story and retelling it using puppets

What to do

◆ Read the story *Goldilocks and the Three Bears*.
◆ Explain to the children that you would like them to make some bear puppets to go with the story.
◆ Give the children brown card and ask them to draw three bears. Remind them that one must be big, one must be medium and one must be small.
◆ Now ask them to cut out the bears and to check they have different size bears.
◆ Attach sticks to the back of the bears using sticky tape or glue.
◆ Now ask the children to use the bear puppets to retell the story. Use a doll for Goldilocks.

Extension activities

◆ Ask the children to make three different size bowls, chairs and beds for the bears.
◆ Make a picnic for the bears and share the food.
◆ Make a hat for the bears.
◆ Make a teddy bear picture using sticky paper shapes.
◆ Invite children to make some porridge. Measure the ingredients needed.
◆ Retell the story from the point of view of different characters (see I am Goldilocks / Baby Bear, pages 53–55).

Link to early learning goals

◆ Use developing mathematical ideas and methods to solve practical problems

Knowledge and Understanding of the World

Children are naturally curious and need to be given opportunities to explore and investigate their world. In this chapter children will develop the knowledge and understanding needed to make sense of their surrounding world. The activities shown here will provide opportunities for children to:

◆ use their senses to explore the world
◆ develop their observation skills
◆ identify the properties of plants and animals and the conditions needed for life
◆ ask questions and acquire new knowledge
◆ expand their vocabulary to be able to talk about the properties of substances
◆ experiment with natural materials
◆ discover how things work
◆ discuss their conclusions with their peers and others
◆ make predictions and test to verify
◆ use a variety of specialised resources, such as magnifying glasses and tape recorders
◆ build and construct using a wide range of materials and tools
◆ understand that they live in a multicultural society and the need to value people equally
◆ be aware of their local surroundings and point out key features.

The early learning goal of Knowledge and Understanding of the World is broken down into 11 learning opportunities, which are listed on the chart on page 99. Each learning opportunity is covered by two or three activities that will help children to achieve that target. The last column on the chart is for comments, and can be used for planning and assessment purposes.

Learning opportunities chart

Learning opportunity	Activities (and page numbers)	Comments
Investigate objects and materials by using all of their senses as appropriate	Kitchen utensil water play (100); Chocolate bird's nest (101); Sensory walk (102–103)	
Find out about, and identify some features of, living things, objects and events they observe	My own garden (104); Butterfly costume (105); Bird food (106)	
Look closely at similarities, differences, patterns and changes	Chocolate bird's nest (101); My own garden (104); Patterned jumper (107–108)	
Ask questions about why things happen and how things work	Kitchen utensil water play (100); Chocolate bird's nest (101)	
Build and construct with a wide range of objects, selecting appropriate resources and adapting their work where necessary	Make a maze (109–111); Supermarket till (112–113); Make a house (114)	
Select the tools and techniques they need to shape, assemble and join the materials they are using	Body puppet (115–116); Picnic food (117)	
Find out about and identify the uses of everyday technology and use information and communication technology and programmable toys to support their learning	Supermarket till (112–113); Interview the family (118–119)	
Find out about past and present events in their own lives, and in those of their families and other people they know	Interview the family (118–119); Me – past and present (120–121)	
Observe, find out about and identify features in the place they live and the natural world	Trip to the park (122); Seaside collage (123); Where we live (124)	
Begin to know about their own cultures and beliefs and those of other people	Pick a country (125–126); International music and dance (127); International food (128–129)	
Find out about their environment, and talk about those features they like and dislike	Trip to the parK (122); Seaside collage (123); School playground (130)	

Kitchen utensil water play

You will need

Water tray; water; a variety of kitchen utensils (sieves, egg beaters, spoons, bottles and jugs, bowls and beakers of various sizes)

Group size

Small groups

What will the children learn?

- ◆ Hand–eye coordination and pre-writing skills
- ◆ To understand how liquids behave, eg it is runny; it doesn't have a shape of its own
- ◆ To understand the mathematical concepts of size and volume

What to do

- ◆ Fill the water tray with water.
- ◆ Provide the children with a wide selection of kitchen utensils.
- ◆ Let them explore and have some fun.
- ◆ Talk to the children and encourage them to notice how water behaves as they scoop, tip and pour it.
- ◆ Encourage the children to ask questions and help them to find the answers.
- ◆ Use different size dishes and ask the children to guess which will hold the most water.

Extension activities

- ◆ Provide other water play equipment such as water wheels, pumps and siphons.
- ◆ Add colour to the water.
- ◆ Put in bubble bath so the children can try to make bubbles.
- ◆ Introduce the terms 'floating' and 'sinking'. Ask the children to investigate.
- ◆ Use sand instead of water and ask children to investigate its properties.

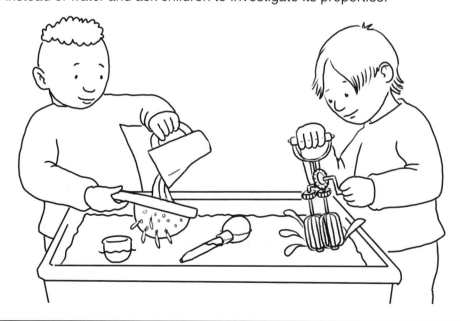

Links to early learning goals

- ◆ Investigate materials by using their senses
- ◆ Ask questions about why things happen

Chocolate bird's nests

You will need

Pictures or videos of bird's nests; 1 chocolate bar; mixing bowl; hot water; box of corn flakes; 2 scooped orange halves; chocolate eggs; bowl and spoon

Group size

Small groups

What will the children learn?

◆ To observe the change in materials, ie chocolate going from solid to liquid
◆ To ask questions
◆ That cooking involves lots of scientific processes: melting, freezing, heating and mixing
◆ Opposites: hot/cold, soft/hard, and wet/dry

What to do

◆ Begin by showing the children pictures and videos of bird's nests.
◆ Explain to children that they are going to make a chocolate bird's nest.
◆ Break the chocolate into pieces.
◆ Put the pieces into a small bowl and melt over a bowl of hot water.
◆ Talk about how the chocolate changes.
◆ Pour in the corn flakes and mix.
◆ Pour the mixture into the orange skin halves.
◆ Place some chocolate eggs on top and place in the fridge.
◆ Ask the children to guess what will happen when the mixture has been put in the fridge.
◆ Once the mixture is hard remove from fridge and take the nests out of the orange halves.
◆ You now have your chocolate bird's nests. Eat and enjoy.

Extension activities

◆ Let the children feel the ingredients before and after they have changed.
◆ Talk to the children about how birds make nests.
◆ Ask the children to try to make a nest out of twigs or straw.
◆ Discuss how birds lay eggs and hatch their young.
◆ Discuss how children can encourage birds to come into their garden.
◆ Put out some bird food and try to identify the birds that come and eat it.
◆ Ask the children to design a bird table.

Links to early learning goals

◆ Investigate materials by using their senses
◆ Look closely at similarities, differences and changes
◆ Ask questions about why things happen

Sensory walk

You will need
Sensory walk sheet (see page 103); pencils; clip boards

Group size
Large groups

What will the children learn?
◆ Observation and investigative skills
◆ To be aware of their senses and use them
◆ Fine motor skills – drawing

What to do
◆ Talk to the children about their senses: sight, hearing, touch, taste, smell.
◆ Show the children the Sensory walk sheet and explain that the pictures represent the senses of sight, hearing, touch and smell.
◆ Explain to the children that they are going for a sensory walk in the outside area and you would like them to use their senses (excluding taste).
◆ Ask children to draw on the sheet what they sensed. For example, in the smell box they could draw a flower; in the touch box they could draw the bark of a tree.
◆ Back in the classroom ask the children to show their work to one another and discuss it.

Extension activities
◆ This activity could be done in a variety of places: in the park, at home, in the classroom, etc.
◆ Investigate the sense of taste during snack time.
◆ Collect items to make a sensory collage (see Seaside collage, page 123).
◆ Ask children to investigate one object using as many of their senses as they can. For example, soap could be investigated using sight, touch and smell.
◆ Read *Spot's Walk in the Woods* by Eric Hill (Picture Puffins).

Link to early learning goals
◆ Investigate objects and materials by using all of their senses as appropriate

Sensory walk sheet

103

My own garden

You will need

Area of ground prepared for planting; garden tools; seeds; long sheets of paper folded like concertinas to make zigzag books; pencils

Group size

Whole class, then small groups

What will the children learn?
◆ Observation skills
◆ To appreciate nature
◆ The growth cycle of a plant
◆ To name the parts of a plant
◆ The conditions a plant needs to grow

What to do

◆ Begin by showing the children the area of ground you will be using.
◆ Explain to the children that this is going to be their own garden.
◆ Ask children to make suggestions as to what they would like to plant.
◆ Write down suggestions and buy the appropriate seeds (go for those that will be quick and easy to grow).
◆ In small groups plant the seeds and water. Point out that seeds need soil, water and sunlight to grow.
◆ Mark where each type of seed is planted.
◆ Organize a rota so that everybody gets a chance to look after the garden.
◆ Get children to record the growth of the plants, week by week in a zigzag book.
◆ Point out features similar to each plant: stem, leaves, roots, etc.
◆ Discuss similarities and differences between the plants.
◆ Let the children enjoy the fruits of their labour.

Extension activities

◆ Compare the similarities and differences between different types of seeds.
◆ Plant the seeds in different conditions, for example, some without water, some in the dark.
◆ Sort some seeds into hoops according to size, colour, shape, etc.
◆ Make a collage using seeds.
◆ Count how many plants they grow, and measure the tallest plant.
◆ Read *Jasper's Beanstalk* by Nick Butterworth and Mike Inkpen (Simon and Schuster).

Links to early learning goals
◆ Find out about, and identify some features of, living things, objects and events they observe
◆ Look carefully at similarities, differences, patterns and changes

Butterfly costume

You will need

Pictures of butterflies; strips of long card to fit around children's heads; pipe cleaners; card; sticky tape; party blowers; egg cartons; strips of card; crêpe paper; paint; paint brushes; felt-tip pens

What will the children learn?

◆ Creativity and imagination
◆ To name the parts of an insect – six legs, wings, antennae
◆ Fine motor skills – cutting, sticking, painting
◆ To observe living things

Group size

Whole class, then small groups

What to do

◆ Begin by showing pictures of butterflies and point out the key features: eyes, antennae, wings, long tongue.
◆ Explain to the children that they are going to make a butterfly costume.
◆ Start by making the headband to fit the child's head.
◆ Ask children to stick on egg cartons for eyes and the pipe cleaners for antennae.
◆ Now make the wings. Use coloured crêpe paper for the wings and attach card strip loops to go over their arms.
◆ Invite the children to draw a symmetrical pattern on the wings.
◆ The children can now dress up as a butterfly.
◆ Give each child a party blower and ask them to pretend it is the butterfly's long tongue.
◆ Get the children to pretend they are flying from one flower to the next drinking nectar.

Extension activities

◆ The costumes could be used for further PE and drama work (see Caterpillar story, page 152).
◆ Have a special butterfly party or minibeast party where the children come dressed up as their favourite minibeast.
◆ Make butterfly fairy cakes.
◆ Talk about symmetry by looking at butterfly wings (see Butterfly pictures, pages 91–92).
◆ Learn about the life cycle of a butterfly.

Link to early learning goals

◆ Find out about, and identify some features of, living things, objects and events they observe

Bird food

You will need

Pictures of common birds; pine cones; peanut butter (NOTE: use warm lard instead if any child has a nut allergy); birdseed; string

Group size

Large groups

What will the children learn?

◆ Observation skills
◆ Bird names and features
◆ To appreciate nature
◆ How to care for animals

What to do

◆ Begin by showing the children pictures of common birds and naming them. Point out key features: beak, feathers, etc.
◆ Ask the children how they could encourage birds to visit the school's outdoor area.
◆ Talk about the food birds eat: seeds, worms, etc.
◆ Explain to children that they are going to make a treat for the birds.
◆ First collect some pine cones.
◆ Spread some peanut butter over the pine cones and then roll the cones in a plate of birdseed.
◆ Tie a piece of string to the cones and hang them on a tree close to the classroom window.
◆ Ask the children to observe the birds that come to eat from the pine cones.
◆ Encourage the children to use the pictures of birds to try to identify them.

Extension activities

◆ Make a bird table.
◆ Make some bird food by mixing warmed lard with birdseed, then leaving it to harden.
◆ Write a poem about birds.
◆ Take photographs and make a book about the birds that visit.
◆ Record some bird sounds with a tape recorder.
◆ Count the number of birds which come each day.

Link to early learning goals

◆ Find out about, and identify some features of, living things, objects and events they observe

Patterned jumper

You will need
Items of clothing with patterns; Jumper outline sheet (see page 108); sponge shapes; paint; dolls or teddies

What will the children learn?
◆ Observation skills – looking closely at patterns
◆ Fine motor skills – printing, cutting, sticking

Group size
Large groups

What to do
◆ Show children the different items of clothing. Discuss the patterns on them. Is there a repeated pattern?
◆ Give each child a copy of the Jumper outline sheet.
◆ Ask them to use sponge shapes to make a repeated pattern on the jumper.
◆ Leave the sheets to dry, then cut out the jumpers.
◆ Finish by sticking the jumpers on to some dolls or teddies and displaying them.

Extension activities
◆ Ask children to bring in patterned clothing from home.
◆ Instead of sponge prints, use different items for printing, such as fruit, potatoes or utensils.
◆ Ask the children to make patterns on pieces of cloth using fabric paints.
◆ Make repeated patterns using beads and thread.
◆ Ask children to look for patterns in different objects in the classroom.
◆ Ask the children to look for patterns in nature, for example on butterfly wings (see Butterfly pictures, pages 91–92).

Link to early learning goals
◆ Look closely at similarities, differences, patterns and changes

Jumper outline sheet

Play Activities for the Early Years
www.brilliantpublications.co.uk

Make a maze

You will need

Pictures of mazes; Mazes 1 and 2 (see pages 110 and 111); chairs; tables; boxes; large pieces of card; string; rope; hoops; pencil and paper to draw maze

What will the children learn?

◆ Listening and speaking skills
◆ To follow instructions
◆ Planning and problem-solving skills
◆ Creativity and imagination
◆ Directions – left and right

Group size

Large groups

What to do

◆ Begin by showing pictures of mazes and the Mazes sheets. Explain how the purpose is to get from one end to the other.
◆ Ask the children to solve the mazes on the sheets.
◆ Show the children the equipment that is available and plan with them how you could make a maze. Include things to crawl under, balance on, etc.
◆ Draw the plan on a large sheet of paper.
◆ Now help children to construct the maze by looking at the plan. Encourage them to adapt their plan if they come across any difficulties.
◆ Finally let children play in the maze and time how quickly they can complete it.

Extension activities

◆ Add things to make the maze more challenging. For example, children could be asked to complete the maze whilst balancing a bean bag on their head.
◆ If possible take a trip to a maze.
◆ Design and make an obstacle course (see Obstacle course, page 96).
◆ Draw some mazes on paper for others to solve.
◆ The children could work in pairs, with one child pretending to be a robot and the other child giving directions to the robot to complete the maze.

Link to early learning goals

◆ Build and construct with a wide range of objects, selecting appropriate resources and adapting their work where necessary

Maze 1

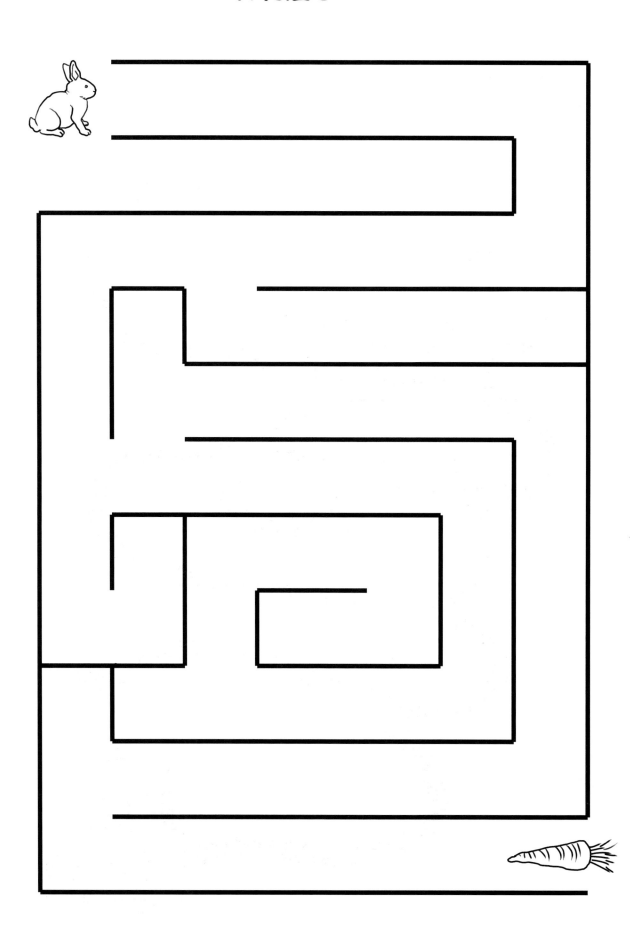

Play Activities for the Early Years
www.brilliantpublications.co.uk

Maze 2

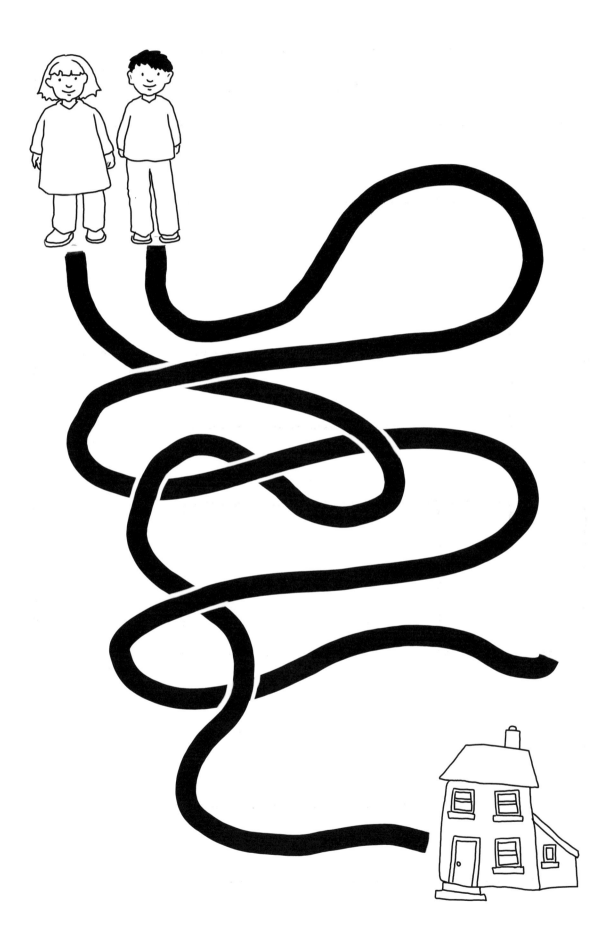

Supermarket till

You will need

Pictures or examples of tills; cardboard boxes and other junk material; paper; paints; glue, sticky tape; scissors; home corner set up as supermarket (see pages 58 and 113 for labels); general grocery items (tins, bottles, cereal boxes, egg boxes, etc)

What will the children learn?

◆ Creativity and imagination
◆ The use of technology in their environment
◆ Using a wide range of resources – selecting what they need and using appropriately
◆ Listening and speaking skills through role play
◆ Cooperation skills in group work

Group size

Whole class, then small groups

What to do

◆ Begin by making a trip to a supermarket.
◆ Point out all the electronic equipment used in the supermarket: tills, bar-code scanners, automatic doors.
◆ If possible, let the children have a try on a till. Point out how the food is scanned, show the receipt, point out what is done with a credit card.
◆ Back in the classroom show pictures or examples of tills. Point out the main features.
◆ Divide the children into small groups and ask them to construct a till using the materials provided. Give guidance and support where needed.
◆ Now use the till in a role play, with one child on the till and others being the customers. Provide a variety of grocery items.

Extension activities

◆ Investigate other electronic equipment used in a supermarket: weighing scales, bar-code scanners, etc.
◆ Ask children to write a shopping list (see Shopping at the Supermarket, pages 57–58).
◆ Find out which country different items come from.
◆ Talk about the different jobs people have in a supermarket: baker, pharmacist, butcher, etc.
◆ Set up the home corner as different shops: a florist's, an optician's, a baker's.
◆ Read *Going Shopping* by Sarah Garland (Atlantic Monthly Press).

Links to early learning goals

◆ Build and construct with a wide range of objects, selecting appropriate resources and adapting their work where necessary
◆ Find out about and identify the uses of everyday technology

Labels for supermarket

bread	cheese
milk	orange juice
chicken	chips
potatoes	cake
apples	biscuits
pears	meat
bananas	butter

Play Activities for the Early Years
www.brilliantpublications.co.uk
This page may be photocopied by the purchasing institution only. 113

Make a house

You will need
Book: *The Three Little Pigs*; pictures of houses; variety of different construction equipment (eg Lego®, Duplo®, wooden building blocks)

Group size
Large groups

What will the children learn?
◆ Different materials and their properties
◆ Features of a house
◆ Fine motor control – building using construction material
◆ Problem-solving – adapting their work

What to do
◆ Begin by reading the story *The Three Little Pigs*. Talk about the materials the pigs used and why the house of bricks was the strongest.
◆ Show the children pictures of houses and discuss the key features: roof, windows, door, etc.
◆ Show the children a variety of construction equipment.
◆ Now ask children to build a house using the construction equipment of their choice.
◆ Help the children to look at the house pictures for reference.
◆ When they have finished ask the children to be the wolf and try to blow their house down.
◆ Ask the children to think of ways to make the house stronger. Can they adapt their design?

Extension activities
◆ Use different materials such as cardboard or wood to make houses.
◆ Look closely at the materials the pigs used and find out why the bricks made the strongest house.
◆ Look at pictures of different houses from around the world and investigate the materials used.
◆ Ask the children to look at the different types of houses they see on the way to school: detached, bungalow, etc.
◆ If possible, visit a building site to see how bricks are used to make walls. A parent with brick-laying skills might be prepared to demonstrate how brick walls are made.
◆ Read *This is our House* by Michael Rosen (Candlewick Press).

Link to early learning goals
◆ Build and construct with a wide range of objects, selecting appropriate resources and adapting their work where necessary

Body puppet

You will need

Plastic skeleton; Body parts sheet photocopied onto card (see page 116); split pins; scissors

Group size

Small groups

What will the children learn?

◆ To name body parts
◆ To sequence parts of the body in the correct order
◆ To understand how the body moves
◆ Fine motor skills – cutting

What to do

◆ Ask the children to name the different parts of the body starting with the head and working down to the feet.
◆ Ask the children to move their arms and legs. Show a skeleton and point out the bones (joints) that help them to move.
◆ Explain to children that they are going to make a body puppet using the Body parts sheet and split pins.
◆ Give each child a copy of the sheet and ask them to cut out the body parts.
◆ Demonstrate how to use a split pin safely and ask children to join the body parts using the pins. Help where needed.
◆ When the puppets are finished let the children experiment with moving the different parts.

Extension activities

◆ Ask children to bring in toys which have movable parts.
◆ Ask children to think of different ways to join the parts of the body.
◆ Sing the song 'Head, Shoulders, Knees and Toes'.
◆ Read *Head, Shoulders, Knees and Toes* by Annie Kubler (Child's Play International).
◆ Use puppets for role play or story-telling (see Puppet theatre, page 33).
◆ Invite the children to use fabric bits to dress up the puppets.

Link to early learning goals

◆ Select the tools and techniques they need to shape, assemble and join the materials they are using

Body parts sheet

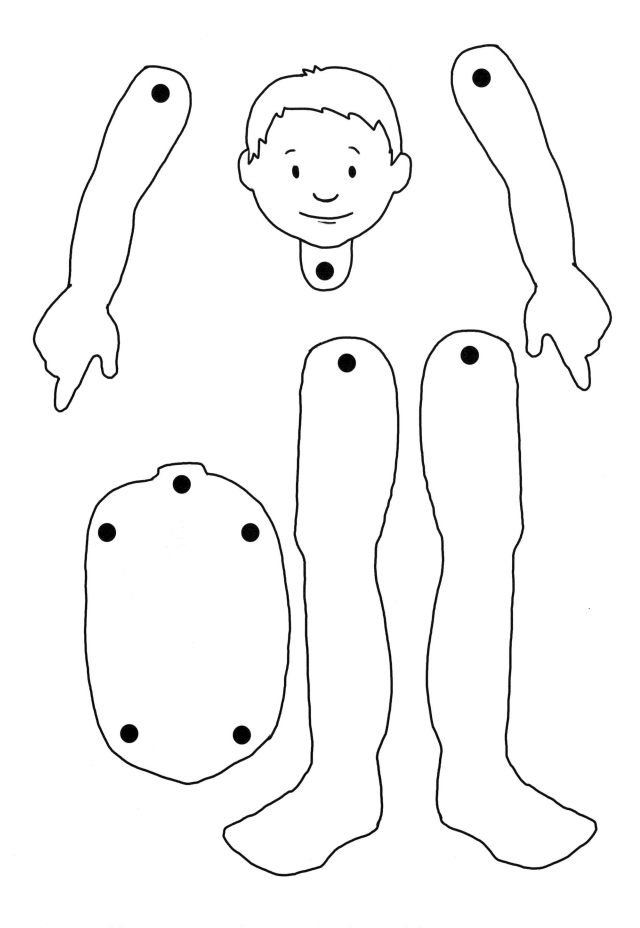

Play Activities for the Early Years
www.brilliantpublications.co.uk

Picnic food

You will need
Blanket; toys; playdough; playdough tools (cutters, blunt knives, spatulas, etc)

Group size
Large groups

What will the children learn?
◆ To use a range of materials and tools
◆ Fine motor skills – using playdough tools
◆ Creativity and imagination
◆ To share
◆ About shape, colour and texture

What to do
◆ Explain to the children that they are going to have a picnic with their toys, but first they need to make some pretend food with playdough.
◆ Ask the children to suggest the food they would like to have on the picnic. Write a list.
◆ Now go through the list and talk about each food: the shape, size, texture, etc. Talk about how they could make the food with playdough. For example, to make sausages they could roll out the playdough using the palm of their hand.
◆ Invite the children to make the different food with the playdough using the tools provided.
◆ Finish by spreading out the blanket and letting the children have a pretend picnic with their toys.

Extension activities
◆ Make food out of other materials: Plasticine, clay, etc.
◆ Count how many toys there are and how much food is needed.
◆ Sort food into hoops according to shape, colour and type.
◆ Ask the children to make a list of the food they want on the picnic.
◆ Make some real picnic food and go on a real picnic.

Link to early learning goals
◆ Select the tools and techniques they need to shape, assemble and join the materials they are using

Interview the family

You will need
Older members of the family; Questions sheet (see page 119); tape recorder; blank tape

Group size
Whole class, then individuals

What will the children learn?
◆ Speaking and listening skills – class discussion and interviewing relatives
◆ To operate a tape recorder independently
◆ To understand the terms 'past' and 'present' and be able to make a comparison
◆ To form good relationships with adults

What to do
◆ Begin by showing children a tape recorder. Explain how to operate it: turn on/off, rewind/ forward, and record.
◆ Ask the children how they could find out what schools were like in the past.
◆ Explain that one way to do this is to talk to older people. Ask them to give examples of people they could talk to.
◆ Explain that you would like them to interview and record on tape an older member of their family about schools in the past.
◆ Show them the Questions sheet and talk about the questions they could ask.
◆ Lend the tape recorder to each child in turn to take home.
◆ Once everyone has recorded their piece play the tape back to the class.
◆ Discuss with the children which things were similar/dissimilar to their school today. Which do they prefer?

Extension activities
◆ Find out when the school was built and find out how it has changed.
◆ Ask parents and grandparents to come in and talk to the children about their schooldays.
◆ Ask the children to find out about other things that have changed over time.

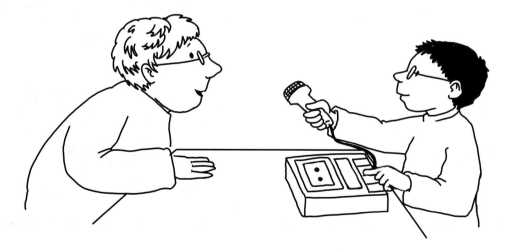

Links to early learning goals
◆ Find out about and identify the uses of everyday technology and use information and communication technology and programmable toys to support their learning
◆ Find out about past and present events in their own lives, and in those of their families and other people they know

Questions sheet

How did you get to school?

What clothes did you wear?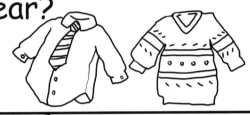

What were your teachers like?

What did you eat for school dinners?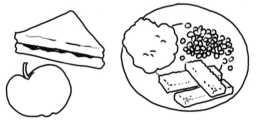

What was your favourite lesson?

Which games did you play in the playground?

Me – past and present

You will need
Photos of children when they were babies and now – doing different activities; Me sheet (see page 121); paper; pencils

Group size
Small groups

What will the children learn?
◆ Observation skills
◆ Listening and speaking skills – discussing their work
◆ To understand and use the terms 'past', 'present' and 'future'
◆ To develop a positive image of themselves

What to do
◆ Ask the children to bring photos from home, some from when they were babies and some from the present time.
◆ Give each child a copy of the Me sheet and explain the words 'past' and 'present'.
◆ Ask the children to stick their baby pictures on the past side and pictures from now on the present side.
◆ Sit in a circle and ask each child to show their work and discuss the differences between each side. Talk about different aspects, such as appearance and ability – when they were babies they crawled, now they can walk and run, etc.

Extension activities
◆ Play a game where you show a baby picture and the children have to guess who it is.
◆ Make a life line.
◆ Ask the children to draw a picture of what they think they will look like in the future.
◆ Ask the children to make a book about themselves.
◆ Show a variety of toys. Ask the children to sort them into baby toys and toys they could play with now.

Link to early learning goals
◆ Find out about past and present events in their own lives, and in those of their families and other people they know

Me

Past

Present

Trip to the park

You will need
Plastic bags; string; sticky tape; plastic coat hangers

Group size
Whole class

What to do

What will the children learn?
◆ Observation skills
◆ To point out features in their local environment
◆ Problem-solving
◆ Creativity and imagination
◆ Fine motor skills
◆ To discuss their likes and dislikes

◆ Talk to the children about a trip to the park and explain that you would like them to collect some natural items such as leaves and twigs.
◆ At the park, ask children to notice different features: the trees, the playground, etc.
◆ Collect the different items in a carrier bag to take back to the classroom.
◆ Back in the classroom, ask children what they observed at the park and what they liked/disliked about it.
◆ Now give the children a coat hanger, sticky tape and string and ask them to construct a park mobile by attaching the items collected to the hanger. Give assistance as necessary.
◆ Display the finished mobile for all to admire.

Extension activities
◆ This activity can be done in different environments, such as the beach, the river. The children could then compare what they found in different places.
◆ This activity can be done in the same place but in different seasons so that the children can see how things change over time.
◆ Paint the items collected before attaching them to the hanger.
◆ Use the items collected in different art work, for example rubbings, prints or collage (see Park collage, page 133).
◆ Read *Spot Goes to the Park* by Eric Hill (Putnam Publishing Group).

Links to early learning goals
◆ Observe, find out about and identify features in the place they live and the natural world
◆ Find out about their environment, and talk about those features they like and dislike

Seaside collage

You will need
Pictures and videos of the seaside; items collected from the seaside (shells, seaweed, pebbles, etc); card; glue

Group size
Whole class

What will the children learn?
◆ Observation skills
◆ To study nature and find out about areas different from their local area
◆ Pattern-making
◆ Creativity and imagination
◆ Increased awareness of environmental issues

What to do
◆ Plan a trip to the seaside or river.
◆ Ask the children to think about what they might see there.
◆ On the trip ask the children to collect different items for collage work, for example shells, seaweed, pebbles.
◆ Back in the classroom ask the children to make a pattern on some card using glue and the things they have collected.
◆ Display and discuss how the seaside differs from the local environment.
◆ Finish by discussing the factors they liked/disliked about the seaside. Are there any things they would like to change?

Extension activities
◆ This activity could be done in different environments and then a comparison could be made between the things found in each place (see Trip to the park, page 122).
◆ The items collected could be used for other art activities such as printing or rubbing.
◆ The activity provides a good opportunity to talk about how we could look after our environment.
◆ Write a class poem about the seaside.

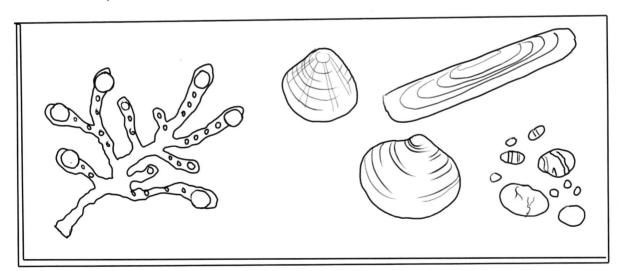

Links to early learning goals
◆ Observe, find out about and identify features in the place they live and the natural world
◆ Find out about their environment, and talk about those features they like and dislike

Where we live

You will need

Simple map of the local area; strips of card; small model buildings and small world toys (cars, people, trees, signs, etc)

Group size

Small groups

What will the children learn?
◆ Observation skills – identify key features
◆ Show an interest in where they live
◆ To follow a plan

What to do
◆ Begin by going for a walk around the local area. Point out key features, for example the post box, doctor's surgery, park.
◆ Back in the classroom show a simple map of the local area.
◆ Explain to the children that you would like them to use the various resources to make a model of the local area.
◆ Help children to lay out strips of card to form roads.
◆ Ask them to use model buildings to mark out the position of key features such as the school, the hospital.
◆ Use small world toys to finish off the town.
◆ Let children have some free play time with the model town.

Extension activities
◆ Use cardboard boxes to make model buildings.
◆ Use other materials to make different items for the model town.
◆ Ask the children to design an imaginary town (see Toy city, page 94).
◆ Count how many buildings there are.
◆ Ask the children to paint pictures of the things they saw on their walk.

Link to early learning goals
◆ Observe, find out about and identify features in the place they live and the natural world

Pick a country

You will need

Globe, magazines, pictures, video, books and CD-ROMs about the chosen country; home corner set up as a travel agent's (see page 126 for labels); large poster-size paper and colour pens

Group size

Whole class, then small groups

What will the children learn?

◆ Increased knowledge of world and country names
◆ About different cultures
◆ Group work and imagination
◆ That information can be gained from different sources: books, videos, etc
◆ To explore the similarities/differences between themselves and other children in the world

What to do

◆ Begin by choosing a country for the week. You could spin a globe and ask a child to close their eyes and point to a country.
◆ Once a country is chosen you and the children can gather information about it.
◆ Have a look at the information and then discuss the similarities/differences between that country and the UK.
◆ Divide the children into small grouops and give each group a large sheet of paper.
◆ Explain that you would like the children to make a poster about the country for display in the home corner (travel agent's). They can draw, or cut and stick pictures from magazines.
◆ Finish by encouraging the children to role play in the home corner. One child could be the travel agent and the others the customers.

Extension activities

◆ Invite people who have lived in or visited the country to come in and talk about it.
◆ Write a list of all the things they would need to pack.
◆ Make a travel brochure about the country.
◆ Design a postcard.

Link to early learning goals

◆ Begin to know about their own cultures and beliefs and those of other people

Labels for travel agent's

holidays	aeroplane
train	ferry
car	world map
countries	travel agent
customer	telephone
computer	travel brochure
tickets	suitcase

 Play Activities for the Early Years
www.brilliantpublications.co.uk

International music and dance

You will need

Tape recorder; taped music from different countries (eg Spain – flamenco, India – bhangra, Caribbean – reggae, South America – tango); pictures/videos of people doing the different dances

What will the children learn?

◆ Link between music and dance
◆ To understand how culture is portrayed in music and dance
◆ Increased knowledge of the world, countries and people
◆ Gross motor skills – move in rhythm with the music
◆ Creativity and imagination

Group size

Whole class

What to do

◆ Begin by playing the music from the different countries.
◆ Show the pictures and videos of people doing the various dances.
◆ Talk about how the music makes them feel. Ask them to move as the music makes them feel.
◆ Show the children some simple dance moves to go with each piece of music.
◆ Encourage them to copy the moves.
◆ Finish by playing a game: play the music and ask the children to guess which country it comes from.

Extension activities

◆ Make costumes to go with each type of music.
◆ Ask children to find out more information about the countries that the music comes from (see Pick a country, pages 125–126).
◆ Have a disco and play music from different countries.
◆ If possible invite people in to demonstrate the real dancing.

Link to early learning goals

◆ Begin to know about their own cultures and beliefs and those of other people

International food

You will need
Chapatti recipe sheet (see page 129); aprons; ingredients for chapattis (see sheet)

Group size
Small groups

What will the children learn?
◆ To name and make different food
◆ About different countries and their food
◆ Basic cooking skills
◆ To taste and express an opinion

What to do
◆ Snack time is a good time to introduce children to food from different countries. NOTE: check for food allergies and restrictions before doing this activity.
◆ Explain to the children that they are going to make some chapattis.
◆ Discuss that chapattis are eaten in India. Show pictures of Indian food.
◆ Ask the children if they have eaten Indian food before.
◆ Ask the children to wash their hands and put on aprons.
◆ Use the Chapatti recipe sheet. Involve the children in the cooking process as much as possible.
◆ Ask children to describe the taste and to say if they like it or not.
◆ For the next snack time make a different dish, from a different country.

Extension activities
◆ Have an international food day where the children can try out different foods from around the world.
◆ Make a bar chart of the children's favourite international food.
◆ Read *Exploring Indian Food* by Sharukh Husain (Mantra Publishing) and *Lima's Red Hot Chilli* by David Mills (Aims International and Books Inc).
◆ Invite people from different communities to show how food is made in their culture.
◆ Show the different utensils people use to eat (eg chopsticks).

Link to early learning goals
◆ Begin to know about their own cultures and beliefs and those of other people

Chapatti recipe sheet

Ingredients

Chapatti flour
Rolling pin
Water
Butter

Equipment

Sieve
Mixing bowl
Frying pan
Knife
Plate
Cup for measuring

What to do

1 Measure out 2 cups of chapatti flour and sift into a bowl. 	2 Add 1 cup of water slowly, mixing and kneading to make a soft dough. 
3 Take small pieces of dough and roll to form small balls, about the size of golf balls. 	4 Use a rolling pin to roll them out into a circle shape. 
5 Place a frying pan on the cooker until hot. 	6 Place a chapatti in the frying pan and cook on both sides. 
7 Turn it out onto a plate. Spread on some butter and let it cool. 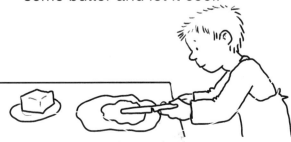	8 Cut the chapatti up into pieces for the children to eat. 

School playground

You will need

Any equipment required to fulfil children's ideas (paint, plants, bins, etc)

Group size

Whole class

What will the children learn?

◆ Observation skills
◆ To express a preference
◆ To care for their environment
◆ Listening and speaking skills – class discussion

What to do

◆ Begin by going for a walk in the school playground or outdoor area.
◆ Back in the classroom talk to the children about their playground. What is the purpose of the playground? Which things do they like/dislike?
◆ Ask the children how they could make the playground better. For example, they might suggest tidy up, paint on games, etc.
◆ Help the children to make some of the changes they suggest.
◆ Afterwards take the children for another walk. Discuss the changes and if they have helped to improve the playground.

Extension activities

◆ Ask the children to draw a design of how they would like the playground to look.
◆ Talk about how the children could care for the environment.
◆ Ask the children to think of games they could play in the playground.
◆ Invite the caretaker/cleaner to talk about how they look after the buildings, etc.
◆ Make some rules for how children should behave in the playground.

Link to early learning goals

◆ Find out about their environments and talk about those features they like and dislike

Creative Development

This chapter shows how to encourage children to use their creative imagination to present their own ideas and experiences in a wide range of media, including music, mimes and gestures, dance, paint, collage and model-making, movement, and stories.

Creative development can help children in many ways and the following activities will give them opportunities to:

◆ use their imagination in real-life and make-believe worlds
◆ respond positively to new experiences
◆ think for themselves independently.

The early learning goal of Creative Development is broken down into five learning opportunities, which are listed on the chart on page 132. Each learning opportunity is covered by between three and five activities that will help children to achieve that target. The last column on the chart is for comments, and can be used for planning and assessment purposes.

Learning opportunities chart

Learning opportunity	Activities (and page numbers)	Comments
Explore colour, texture, shape, form and space in two and three dimensions	Park collage (133); Textured pictures (134); Sand pictures (135); Painting fun (136); Caterpillar fun (148)	
Recognize and explore how sounds can be changed, sing simple songs from memory, recognize repeated sounds and sound patterns and match movements to music	Guess the musical instrument (137); Painting to music (138); The Very Hungry Caterpillar (139)	
Respond in a variety of ways to what they see, hear, smell, touch and feel	Park collage (133); Stained glass pictures (140); Feeling faces (141–142); A snowy day (143–144)	
Use their imagination in art and design, music, dance, imaginative and role play, and stories	Painting fun (136); Painting to music (138); The Very Hungry Caterpillar (139); Florist's shop (145–147)	
Express and communicate their ideas, thoughts and feelings by using a widening range of materials, suitable tools, imaginative and role play, movement, designing and making, and a variety of songs and musical instruments	Painting fun (136); Caterpillar fun (148); Move to the music (149)	

132 **Play Activities for the Early Years**
www.brilliantpublications.co.uk

Park collage

You will need
Plastic bags; card; glue

Group size
Whole class

What will the children learn?
◆ Creativity and imagination
◆ Observation skills and using all their senses
◆ Pattern-making
◆ Self-confidence to discuss their work

What to do
◆ Explain to the children that they are going on a trip to a park to collect different items such as leaves, twigs and stones for some collage work.
◆ During the trip encourage children to use all their senses. Ask them to smell the flowers; ask them to close their eyes and listen to what they can hear; ask them to feel the bark of a tree.
◆ Back in the classroom look at the things collected. Discuss the colour, shape and texture of each thing.
◆ Give each child a piece of card and ask them to make a collage using the things collected.
◆ Encourage the children to use their imagination.
◆ Finish the activity by playing a game where one child is blindfolded and then feels another child's collage picture and tries to guess the items on it.

Extension activities
◆ Use items collected for other art work, such as nature mobiles, 3D models, rubbings, and prints (see Trip to the park, page 122).
◆ Go for a minibeast hunt in the park.
◆ Write a poem/story about the trip to the park.
◆ Count the number of each object they collected.
◆ Make a book about their trip and stick in some of the things they collected.
◆ Read *Spot Goes to the Park* by Eric Hill (Putnam Publishing Group).

Links to early learning goals
◆ Explore colour, texture, shape, form and space in two and three dimensions
◆ Respond in a variety of ways to what they see, hear, smell, touch and feel

Textured pictures

You will need

Clear glue; cardboard box; sand, salt and sawdust – all in shakers; paper; paint brushes

Group size

Large groups

What to do

◆ Invite the children to draw a simple picture. Chose a theme if it helps children to focus, for example a picture of the seaside.

◆ Ask the children to paint glue all over the picture.

◆ Now using the shakers show children how to shake sand, salt and sawdust onto different parts of the picture.

◆ Tip any surplus into a box.

◆ Now ask the children to feel the picture and talk about the different textures. Introduce descriptive words such as 'rough', 'smooth' and 'sharp'.

Extension activities

◆ Invite children to feel the sand, salt and sawdust and to try to describe how they feel.

◆ Use sand, salt and sawdust in other art work.

◆ Mix sand, salt and sawdust with water and observe what happens.

◆ Take an empty bottle. How many cups of sand, salt or sawdust are needed to fill it?

◆ Fill a tray with sand, salt or sawdust. Let children have some free play fun.

What will the children learn?

◆ Listening and speaking skills – to follow instructions and describe their work

◆ Creativity and imagination

◆ To develop the sense of feel and touch

◆ New vocabulary

◆ To use different materials

Link to early learning goals

◆ Explore colour, texture, shape, form and space in two and three dimensions

Sand pictures

You will need
Cardboard; pencils; glue; water; paint brushes; coloured sand

Group size
Large groups

What will the children learn?
◆ Fine motor skills – practising using a finger–thumb grip when sprinkling the sand
◆ To develop their tactile ability
◆ Use of texture and colour
◆ Creativity and imagination

What to do
◆ Explain to children that they are going to make pictures using sand.
◆ Give each child a piece of cardboard.
◆ Ask the children to draw a simple picture (large and not too detailed).
◆ Make a mixture of glue and water (about half as much water as glue).
◆ Ask the children to paint a layer of glue just where they want one of the colours of sand to go.
◆ Ask them to sprinkle sand onto that area. Leave to dry and then tap off any excess sand.
◆ Now paint glue on a different area and sprinkle on a different colour.
◆ Repeat until the picture is finished.
◆ When it is completed, ask the children to feel their picture and describe it.

Extension activities
◆ Instead of sand use different materials such as sawdust, lentils, pasta shapes or dried beans (see Textured pictures, page 134).
◆ If you do not have different coloured sand, use plain sand and paint with tempera paints.
◆ Put some sand in large tray and let children enjoy playing with it. Talk about its properties (it can be poured, it doesn't retain its shape).
◆ Add water to the sand and let children make sand castles.

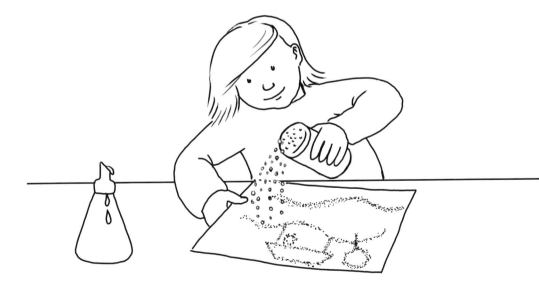

Link to early learning goals
◆ Explore colour, texture, shape, form and space in two and three dimensions

Painting fun

You will need

Cotton buds, feathers, rollers, twigs, sticks, string, sponges, etc; paint; pots; paper; splash mat

Group size

Large groups

What to do

◆ Explain to the children that they are going to do a painting using a wide variety of tools instead of paint brushes.
◆ Lay a splash mat on the floor.
◆ Pour some poster paint into the pots.
◆ Limit the number of colours to three or four to help the children to focus.
◆ Ask the children to choose one item to paint with.
◆ Give the children the paint pots and paper and let them paint.
◆ On your own paper demonstrate how to make dots and swirls using the various tools.
◆ Now ask the children to choose another item and paint with that.
◆ Ask the children which item they preferred painting with.
◆ Finish by displaying the pictures with the tools they used.

Extension activities

◆ Use different types of paint: watercolours, fabric paints, etc.
◆ Add things to the paint to make different textures: sand, sawdust, etc.
◆ Provide different types of paper to paint on: tissue paper, card, crêpe paper, etc.
◆ Invite the children to paint on different items: boxes, rocks, balloons, etc.
◆ Encourage the children to describe their work using a wide range of vocabulary.
◆ Invite the children to paint on a large scale using poster-size paper and large paint brushes.

Links to early learning goals

◆ Explore colour, texture, shape, form and space in two and three dimensions
◆ Use their imagination in art and design
◆ Express and communicate their ideas, thoughts and feelings by using a widening range of materials and suitable tools

Guess the musical instrument

You will need
A variety of musical instruments (eg recorder, guitar, flute, and triangle)

What will the children learn?
◆ Listening and speaking skills
◆ Instrument names and their sounds

Group size
Large groups and eventually whole class

What to do
◆ Sit the children in a circle.
◆ Begin by showing and naming each instrument.
◆ Play each instrument in turn to familiarize the children with the sounds.
◆ Place the instruments in the centre of the circle.
◆ Ask one child to close their eyes and choose another child to go to the centre and play one of the instruments.
◆ The first child has to guess which instrument was played.
◆ Repeat so all children get a turn being a player and a guesser.

Extension activities
◆ Instead of using musical instruments you could use household items that make a sound.
◆ Adapt the game by giving an instrument to a child and then clapping a simple sound pattern that the child has to copy and play back on the instrument.
◆ Sing a common song and get children to play instruments to accompany it.
◆ Use instruments to accompany a story.

Link to early learning goals
◆ Recognize and explore how sounds can be changed, sing simple songs from memory, recognize repeated sounds and sound patterns and match movements to music

Painting to music

You will need

Tape recorder; paper; paints; paint brushes; two different pieces of music, one slow and downbeat, the other fast and upbeat

Group size

Whole class

What will the children learn?

◆ Creativity and imagination
◆ Listening skills
◆ To understand how different emotions can be expressed in music
◆ To express their own emotions

What to do

◆ Ask the children to close their eyes and listen to some music.
◆ Play the first piece of music and ask them to think how it makes them feel. Does it make them feel happy or sad? Does it make them feel energetic or sleepy?
◆ Give each child a piece of paper and paints.
◆ Play the music again and ask children to paint how the music makes them feel. What colour does it make them think of?
◆ Emphasize that the picture should not be of specific items. It should be of patterns and different colours.
◆ Now play the second piece of music and do the activity again.
◆ Finish by comparing the two pictures. Did they use different colours and patterns?
◆ Now let children compare their paintings with those of their peers. Did they use similar colours and patterns?
◆ Display the pairs of paintings with a label indicating the piece of music that is being interpreted.

Extension activities

◆ Ask the children to compose a piece of music that makes them happy/sad.
◆ Talk about other emotions that are expressed in music.
◆ Play some music and ask the children to move their body according to how the music makes them feel (see Move to the music, page 149).

Links to early learning goals

◆ Recognize and explore how sounds can be changed, sing simple songs from memory, recognize repeated sounds and sound patterns and match movements to music
◆ Use their imagination in art and design, music, dance, imaginative and role play, and stories

The Very Hungry Caterpillar

You will need
Storybook: *The Very Hungry Caterpillar* by Eric Carle (Puffin Books); musical instruments

Group size
Whole class

What will the children learn?
◆ To listen carefully – to the story and the instruments
◆ Creativity and imagination – role play being a caterpillar
◆ Instrument names and sounds
◆ Life cycle of a butterfly
◆ Gross motor skills – to move with imagination

What to do
◆ Begin by reading the book *The Very Hungry Caterpillar*.
◆ Show the musical instruments. Name and play each one in turn.
◆ Read the story again and ask the children which instrument would fit in best with each part of the story.
◆ Choose some children to play the instruments as the story is read out.
◆ Now ask the children to pretend they are the caterpillar and to act out each part as it is read. For example:
  ❖ start as a ball on the floor for the beginning
  ❖ slither on the floor like a caterpillar
  ❖ eat the food and get fatter
  ❖ roll up into a cocoon
  ❖ fly away as a butterfly.
◆ Finish by putting the actions and the instruments together. Have some children play the instruments whilst others act out the story, and then swap.

Extension activities
◆ Make costumes and masks to go with the story (see Butterfly costume, page 105).
◆ Mount a display about the life cycle of a butterfly (see Caterpillar story, page 152).
◆ Use a variety of art resources and different techniques to make caterpillars and butterflies.
◆ Look at other minibeasts and play instruments to express their movements.

Links to early learning goals
◆ Recognize and explore how sounds can be changed, sing simple songs from memory, recognize repeated sounds and sound patterns and match movements to music
◆ Use their imagination in art and design, music, dance, imaginative and role play, and stories

Stained glass pictures

You will need

Pictures of stained glass windows; thin paper; pencils; glue in a bottle with a pointed nozzle; crayons; felt-tip pens

What will the children learn?

◆ Observation skills
◆ Creativity and imagination
◆ Fine motor control – drawing, gluing and colouring in

Group size

Whole class

What to do

◆ Take the children to visit a local church.
◆ Encourage the children to observe using all their senses: look at the colours in the stained glass windows, smell the candles, listen to the organ, etc.
◆ Back in the classroom show the children pictures of stained glass windows.
◆ Point out the key features: the use of lines to break up the picture, the bright colours, the effect created when the light shines through.
◆ Explain to children that they are going to make some stained glass pictures.
◆ Begin by asking the children to draw a simple picture on a piece of thin paper.
◆ Emphasize that the picture must be large and not too detailed (eg a house).
◆ Now ask them to draw lines to divide their drawings into pieces like a stained glass window.
◆ Squeeze a line of glue along the lines on the picture to outline each big shape. Leave to dry.
◆ When the glue is dry, colour in each area with crayons or felt-tip pens.
◆ Finish by displaying pictures on a window so the sun shines through.

Extension activities

◆ Use different materials. For example, you could use strips of black paper for the lines and crêpe paper for the coloured pieces.
◆ Discuss the material used in real stained glass windows: lead, glass, etc.
◆ Discuss what a church is and what happens there.
◆ Look at other places of worship.
◆ Choose a stained glass window. Look at the picture and make up a story about it.
◆ Count how many stained glass windows were in the church.

Link to early learning goals

◆ Respond in a variety of ways to what they see, hear, smell, touch and feel

Feeling faces

You will need
Faces sheet (see page 142); cards with different scenarios

Group size
Whole class

What will the children learn?
- To express and understand emotions
- Self-awareness
- To communicate by using their body
- To observe, imitate and act

What to do
- Begin by explaining to the children that you are going to show them pictures of faces of different emotions, such as happy, sad and excited (see Faces sheet).
- Show a sad face and ask children to guess what the person is feeling. Ask them to think of different things that make them sad and to talk about these.
- Do the same for the other faces and emotions.
- Now explain to children that you are going to describe a situation and you want the children to show how they would feel. Possible scenarios include:
  - ❖ you have lost your cat
  - ❖ it is your birthday
  - ❖ you are watching a scary film.
- Now ask a child to take your place and describe a different situation.
- For younger children, model the type of facial expressions they could do.
- For older children, encourage them to show by their movements and actions how they would feel.

Extension activities
- Cut out pictures in magazines which show different expressions.
- Ask the children to make a book about things that make them happy, sad, angry, etc.
- Have a quiet corner where children can sit and calm down if they feel sad or angry.
- Play a guessing game where one child mimes an emotion and the other children have to guess what it is.
- Read *Copycat Faces* (Dorling Kindersley Publishing).

Link to early learning goals
- Respond in a variety of ways to what they see, hear, smell, touch and feel

Faces sheet

happy

sad

angry

frightened

excited

tired

This page may be photocopied by the purchasing institution only.

A snowy day

You will need

Snowman cut-out (see page 144); cotton wool; buttons; twigs; paper; wool; glue

Group size

Whole class, then large groups

What will the children learn?

◆ Observing using all of their senses
◆ Fine motor skills – cutting and gluing

What to do

◆ Begin by taking children for a walk on a snowy day.
◆ On the walk ask children to use all their senses: feel the snow with their hands and feet; let a snowflake fall in their mouth; look at what snowflakes look like; listen to what sound the snow makes under their feet.
◆ If there is enough snow make a snowman.
◆ Back in the classroom give each child a snowman cut-out.
◆ Ask them to use the resources available to make a snowman.
◆ Display the finished results for all to admire.

Extension activities

◆ Watch the video *The Snowman* (Universal Pictures Video).
◆ Watch what happens to snow when it melts, then put it into a freezer and see what happens.
◆ Make a snowy day picture on the computer.
◆ Ask the children to make up a story about their snowman and record it on a tape.
◆ Read *Zoe's Snowy Day* by Barbara Reid (Scholastic).

Link to early learning goals

◆ Respond in a variety of ways to what they see, hear, smell, touch and feel

Snowman cut-out

This page may be photocopied by the purchasing institution only.

Florist's shop

You will need

Home corner set up as a florist's shop (see pages 146 and 147 for labels); flowers made of a variety of materials (plastic, silk, paper, etc); baskets; pots; ribbon; tissue paper; till; play money; note pads; pens; play phone

What will the children learn?

◆ Role play – imagination
◆ Listening and speaking skills – during role play
◆ To see the world from another person's point of view

Group size

Small groups

What to do

◆ Talk with children about a florist's shop and the different things the florist does: make bouquets, take phone calls, deliver flowers.
◆ Talk about all the different occasions flowers are given: birthdays, baby's birth, Valentine's day, etc.
◆ Now invite the children to play in the florist's shop. Two children can be the florists and the rest can be customers.
◆ Help model behaviour by being the florist first and then the customer. Ask appropriate questions. Which flowers would you like? Can I have the address it is going to?
◆ Allow all the children to have turns being a florist and a customer.

Extension activities

◆ Turn the home corner into different types of shops. Possibilities include an optician's, a clothes shop, a supermarket, a shoe shop or a pet store (see Hospital home corner, pages 12–13, and Shopping at the supermarket, pages 57–58).
◆ Ask children to memorize their address and phone number. Encourage them to recite their address when ordering flowers.
◆ Ask the children to try to write names and addresses down.
◆ Make flowers using a variety of resources.
◆ Use play money to pay for the flowers.

Link to early learning goals

◆ Use their imagination in art and design, music, dance, imaginative role play, and stories

Labels for florist's shop 1

florist	customer
special offer	till
flowers for sale	open
pot	basket
seeds	soil
bouquets	telephone
Congratulations	Happy Birthday

Labels for florist's shop 2

Valentine's Day	For the birth of a baby
tulips 1p	daffodils 2p
lilies 3p	snowdrops 4p
roses 5p	carnations 6p

Caterpillar fun

You will need

Pictures of caterpillars; for Caterpillar 1 – egg boxes, paint, glue, scissors, paint brushes; for Caterpillar 2 – cotton wool, stockings, elastic bands, fabric paints, paint brushes; for Caterpillar 3 – Plasticine and playdough

What will the children learn?

◆ Creativity and imagination
◆ Fine motor skills – cutting, gluing, painting
◆ About the features of a caterpillar
◆ To use a range of resources and tools in their art work

Group size

Whole class

What to do

◆ Show the children pictures of caterpillars and point out key features: long body divided into segments, the colours and patterns, etc.
◆ Explain that they are going to make caterpillars using different materials:

❖ **Caterpillar 1**
Give children the egg boxes and ask them to cut them up into individual units. Now glue the pieces together in a long line. Paint (using pictures of caterpillars for reference) and leave to dry.

❖ **Caterpillar 2**
Ask the children to stuff some cotton wool into a stocking. Tie elastic bands to make segments. Now paint using fabric paints – use pictures for reference.

❖ **Caterpillar 3**
Give the children playdough and Plasticine and ask them to roll out to make caterpillars.

◆ Finish by displaying the different caterpillars in a setting of paper leaves.

Extension activities

◆ Read *The Crunching, Munching Caterpillar* by Sheridan Cain and Jack Tickle (Tiger Tales).
◆ Learn how the caterpillar changes into a butterfly.
◆ Make up a class story about a caterpillar (see The Very Hungry Caterpillar, page 139, and Caterpillar story, page 152).

Links to early learning goals

◆ Explore colour, texture, shape, form and space in two and three dimensions
◆ Express and communicate their ideas, thoughts and feelings by using a widening range of materials, suitable tools, imaginative and role play, movement, designing and making, and a variety of songs and musical instruments

Move to the music

You will need
Video of people dancing with different items (eg gymnasts dancing with ribbons); tape of different types of music; ribbons; scarves; sticks; streamers; balls

Group size
Whole class

What will the children learn?
◆ Understand that music can reflect different feelings
◆ Gross motor skills – moving with different items
◆ Coordination
◆ Creativity and imagination – moving to the music

What to do
◆ Begin by showing the children a video of people dancing with different items.
◆ Explain to the children that you are going to play some music and then ask them to move to it using different items.
◆ Play the music and ask them how the music makes them feel. Ask them how they could reflect these feelings in their movements.
◆ Give each child a ribbon and ask them how they could move to the music using the ribbon; for example, twirling around, running and trailing the ribbon behind them.
◆ Ask children to find a space. Now play the music again and ask them to move to the music using the ribbon.
◆ You may have to model what to do, or choose children to show their ideas to the rest of the class.
◆ Now play a different type of music and give children a different item (eg a scarf).
◆ Carry on until the children have used all the items.
◆ Finish by letting the children choose their favourite item and having some free play time.

Extension activities
◆ Make different items for the children to dance with, for example batons or streamers.
◆ Talk about different feelings (see Happy/sad masks, pages 22–24, and Feeling faces, pages 141–142). What makes them happy/sad, etc?
◆ Ask the children to use musical instruments to compose some music for other children to move to.
◆ Count how many different items the children dance with.

Link to early learning goals
◆ Express and communicate their ideas, thoughts and feelings by using a widening range of materials, suitable tools, imaginative and role play, movement, designing and making, and a variety of songs and musical instruments

Physical Development

In this chapter children gain knowledge and understanding of their bodies and build confidence in themselves. The activities provide opportunities for children to:

◆ develop hand–eye coordination
◆ increase physical fitness, strength and stamina
◆ use movements to express feelings and respond to music
◆ gain knowledge about their bodies
◆ develop their gross and fine motor skills
◆ use space confidently
◆ become confident to try new skills and challenging tasks.

The early learning goal of Physical Development is broken down into eight learning opportunities, which are listed on the chart on page 151. Each learning opportunity is covered by between two and four activities that will help children to achieve that target. The last column on the chart is for comments, and can be used for planning and assessment purposes.

Learning opportunity chart

Learning opportunity	Activities (and page numbers)	Comments
Move with confidence and imagination, and in safety	Caterpillar story (152); Minibeast safari (153)	
Move with control and coordination	Bean bag games (154); Trolley dash (155); Traffic light game (156)	
Show awareness of space, of themselves and others	Skittle fun (157); Easy Catch (158); Musical Cushions (159); Relaxation time (160)	
Recognize the importance of keeping healthy and those things which contribute to this	Is it healthy? (161); Healthy teeth (162–163); Healthy food plate (164)	
Recognize the changes that happen to their bodies when they are active	Traffic light game (156); Relaxation time (160)	
Use a range of small and large equipment	Bean bag games (154); Trolley dash (155); Skittle fun (157); Easy Catch (158)	
Travel around, under, over and through balancing and climbing equipment	Going on a Bear Hunt (165); Grand Old Duke of York (166)	
Handle tools, objects, and construction and malleable materials safely and with increasing control	Clay pot (167); Papier mâché ladybirds (168)	

Caterpillar story

You will need
Book: *The Very Hungry Caterpillar* by Eric Carle (Puffin Books); reference books and videos about the life cycle of butterflies

Group size
Whole class

What to do
◆ Begin by reading the book about the hungry caterpillar and talk about how he changed to a butterfly.
◆ Show reference books and videos about the life cycle of a butterfly.
◆ Tell the children that they are going to pretend they are a caterpillar and change into a butterfly.
◆ Start by asking children to roll up tight like an egg on a leaf.
◆ Now, pop!, they come out as a caterpillar.
◆ Ask children to slither along the ground like a caterpillar eating its food.
◆ Now they are fat and move along very slowly.
◆ They go into their cocoon and go to sleep.
◆ Next they try to break through the cocoon and come out as a butterfly.
◆ They stretch out their wings and flutter them slowly to let them dry.
◆ Finally they can fly off like a butterfly.

Extension activities
◆ You can do the same activity for different life cycles, for example of a frog or a dragonfly.
◆ Make costumes and perform to another class (see Butterfly costume, page 105).
◆ Make caterpillars and butterflies in art work using a variety of resources and techniques.
◆ Count how many things the caterpillar eats on each day.
◆ Learn the days of the week. Help the children to make a weekly calendar. Ask them to draw one activity that they do on each day.
◆ Act out the story (see The Very Hungry Caterpillar, page 139).

Link to early learning goals
◆ Move with confidence and imagination, and in safety

Minibeast safari

You will need
Books, videos and pictures of minibeasts

Group size
Whole class

What will the children learn?
- To move with imagination
- To follow instructions
- Role play
- Gross motor skills
- To identify and name various minibeasts

What to do
- Show the children the information about different minibeasts.
- Discuss with them how different minibeasts move around:
  - spiders – scurry around very fast
  - butterflies – fly gracefully
  - bees – buzz from one flower to the next
  - ants – march in a line
  - worms – wiggle through the earth
  - grasshoppers – leap around.
- Now call out the name of a minibeast and ask the children to move like that minibeast. For example, if you call out 'Butterfly', they should fly gracefully from one flower to the next; if you call out 'Spider', they should spin a web.
- Finish by sitting in a circle. Ask one child to pretend to be a minibeast; the other children have to guess what it is.

Extension activities
- Ask the children to make costumes of minibeasts and have a minibeast theme party.
- Look for and observe minibeasts in the garden.
- Make different minibeasts out of playdough.
- Count the number of legs each minibeast has.
- Sort plastic minibeasts into hoops: by colour, number of legs, etc.

Link to early learning goals
- Move with confidence and imagination, and in safety

Bean bag games

You will need
Bean bags; skittles; hoop; bucket; obstacle course equipment

Group size
Whole class

What will the children learn?
- Hand–eye coordination
- Gross motor skills
- Group cooperation
- Balance

What to do
- Explain to children that they are going to play a couple of different games using a bean bag:
  - **Game 1**
    Ask the children to balance a bean bag on their hand and walk from one side of the room to the other. Now balance it on their foot and walk again. Now balance on their head … and so on.
  - **Game 2**
    Put the children in pairs and ask them to practise throwing and catching the bean bag.
  - **Game 3**
    Put up some skittles and ask the children to try to knock them down using the bean bags.
  - **Game 4**
    Place a bucket a short distance from the children and ask them to try to throw the bean bags into it.
  - **Game 5**
    Set up an obstacle course and ask children to do the course with a bean bag on their head.
  - **Game 6**
    Put a hoop a short distance away and ask children to throw the bean bags into it.

Extension activities
- Do the same activity but with a ball rather than a bean bag.
- Make a bean bag. Put some dried beans into a plastic bag and seal. Make a bag out of felt and put the plastic bag of beans inside and sew shut.

Links to early learning goals
- Move with control and coordination
- Use a range of small and large apparatus

Trolley dash

You will need
Toy trolleys or prams; chalk; cones; play grocery items

Group size
Large groups

What will the children learn?
◆ To follow a route
◆ Gross motor skills – pushing and pulling
◆ Control and coordination

What to do
◆ Use chalk to mark out a route and place cones on the route as obstacles.
◆ Mark out about four routes with a start and finish line.
◆ Place some play grocery items along various parts of each route.
◆ Give each child a toy trolley or pram.
◆ Explain to the children that they will need to push their trolley along the route, going carefully around the cones, picking up and placing the grocery items in the trolley and running to the finish line.
◆ Explain to the children that the aim is not to be first across the finish line but to stick as closely as possible to the route.
◆ Line up the children and start them off.

Extension activities
◆ Set different tasks along the way; for example, put on a coat, balance a bean bag on their head.
◆ Put extra weight in the trolley. Does this make it easier or harder to push?
◆ Make a trolley out of boxes and string and ask the children to pull it along.
◆ Play with other wheeled toys: scooters, tricycles, bicycles, pull-along carts, etc.

Links to early learning goals
◆ Move with control and coordination
◆ Use a range of small and large equipment

Traffic light game

You will need
Large open space; stethoscope

Group size
Whole class

What will the children learn?
- Listening skills
- To follow instructions
- Gross motor control
- Increasing awareness of their body

What to do
- Explain to the children the rules for the traffic light game: red means stop, amber means walk and green means run.
- Remind the children that when they are running about they must ensure they do not bump into one another.
- Begin by asking the children to try to listen to their heart when sitting quietly. Show them how to do this with their fingers or use a stethoscope.
- Now play the game. Shout out the different colours and the children respond appropriately.
- Now ask the children to stop and try to listen to their heart again.
- Ask them what differences they noticed in their body before and after playing the game: fast pulse, sweaty, red face, etc.

Extension activities
- Play the same game but use different words. For example, you could use fruit names – banana means stop, etc.
- Make the game more complex by adding more words and actions, for example blue means jump up and down, purple means hop around, etc.
- Let the children have turns shouting out the colours.
- Play other games: Musical Statues, Knives and Forks, etc.

Links to early learning goals
- Move with control and coordination
- Recognize the changes that happen to their bodies when they are active

Skittle fun

You will need
Empty plastic bottles with lids; sand; balls; paint; paint brushes; pcn; chalk

Group size
Small groups

What will the children learn?
- Fine motor skills – pouring sand into the bottles
- Gross motor skills – throwing balls
- To count from 1 to 10

What to do
- Explain to the children that they are going to make a skittles game.
- Ask them to pour the sand into about 10 bottles.
- Decorate the bottles and paint on numbers 1 to 10.
- Decide with the children how far apart the skittles should be and how far away the children should stand. Mark with chalk.
- Set the bottles in a triangular pattern.
- Now you are ready to play.
- Ask the children to stand behind the line and throw a ball to try to knock down as many skittles as they can.
- Count how many each child knocks down.
- Ask children to count how many are knocked down and how many are left standing in each turn.

Extension activities
- Instead of skittles and balls, use toilet roll tubes and bean bags.
- Do basic subtraction/addition using skittles. Count how many have been knocked down. Take away from 10 to find how many are left (see Skittle game, page 87).
- Practise number bonds by working out how many skittles have been knocked down and how many are still standing.
- Play different games using the bottles and a ball.

Links to early learning goals
- Show awareness of space, of themselves and others
- Use a range of small and large apparatus

Easy Catch

You will need
Old oven mitts; felt; self-adhesive Velcro®; glue; tennis balls

Group size
Pairs

What will the children learn?
◆ Gross motor skills – throwing and catching
◆ Cooperation – working in pairs
◆ A sense of space – that they must stand a certain distance apart

What to do
◆ Explain to children they are going to make a catching game called 'Easy Catch'.
◆ Start by asking the children to stick Velcro® to the tennis balls.
◆ Now ask them to glue felt to the oven mitts.
◆ Everything is now ready to play Easy Catch.
◆ Divide the children into pairs.
◆ Decide how far apart the children should stand and mark with chalk if necessary.
◆ One person throws the ball and the other tries to catch it with the oven mitt on.
◆ The Velcro® should stick to the mitt.
◆ Let the children then swap places with each other.

Extension activities
◆ Increase the distance between the catcher and thrower to make the game more difficult.
◆ Play catch using other items such as bean bags (see Bean bag games, page 154).
◆ Count how many times they catch the ball without dropping it.

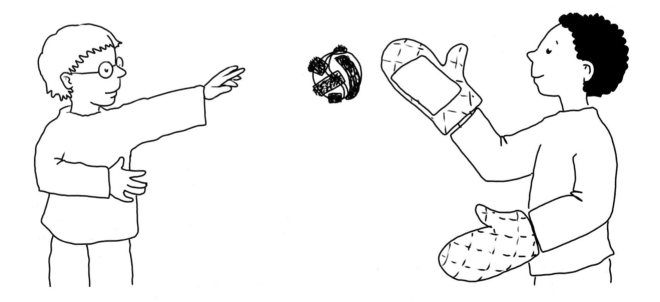

Links to early learning goals
◆ Show awareness of space, of themselves and others
◆ Use a range of small and large apparatus

Musical Cushions

You will need

Cushions; music; tape recorder

Group size

Large groups

What to do

- Begin by explaining the rules of Musical Cushions. When the music is on the children must dance around and when the music stops they must sit on a cushion.
- Emphasize that when children are dancing they must not bump into each other and must move around the room.
- Start by asking children to find a space. Show them how to check they have enough space by spreading their arms out wide and turning in a circle. If they touch anyone else they need to move.
- Play the game and remove one cushion on each turn. The winner is the last child left in the game.

What will the children learn?

- How to find a space
- To be aware of others
- Gross motor control – dancing and stopping
- Listening and concentration skills

Extension activities

- Play Musical Statues or Musical Chairs.
- Count how many cushions there are and ask the children how many will be left if one is removed.
- Play different types of music and ask the children to move accordingly (see Painting to music, page 138, and Move to the music, page 149).
- Rather than a tape of music, ask a child to play a musical instrument and stop when they want the other children to sit down.

Link to early learning goals

- Show awareness of space, of themselves and others

Relaxation time

You will need
Tape of soothing music

Group size
Whole class

What will the children learn?
◆ To understand the term 'relaxation'
◆ To name body parts
◆ To observe the changes in their body when active and when relaxed

What to do
◆ Try to do this activity the same time every day: the start of the day, the end of the day, before lunch time, at the end of a PE lesson, etc.
◆ Explain to the children that they are going to have some relaxation time.
◆ Discuss what the word 'relaxation' means – to wind down and rest their mind and body.
◆ Ask the children to lie on the floor and close their eyes. Ask them to make sure they have their own space and cannot touch anyone else.
◆ Stress the importance of keeping quiet and still.
◆ Put on a tape of soothing music.
◆ Ask the children to start by tensing their body and then relaxing it.
◆ Go through each part of the body, starting with the feet and ending with the face, tensing and relaxing.
◆ Explain what the term 'tensing' means – squeezing and tightening.
◆ Finish by letting the children lie still and listen to the music for a minute or two.
◆ Ask the children to open their eyes and sit up slowly.
◆ Talk about how the children feel before and after the session. Discuss how their body feels when they are active and how it feels when they are resting.

Extension activities
◆ Invite the children to compose their own relaxation music.
◆ Ask children to do an activity such as painting before and after the relaxation session. Did it make any difference to how they did the activity?
◆ Measure the difference in the children's heart beat before and after relaxation time (see Traffic light game, page 156).

Links to early learning goals
◆ Show awareness of space, of themselves and others
◆ Recognize the changes that happen to their bodies when they are active

Is it healthy?

You will need

Healthy food: fruit, vegetables, brown bread, pure juices, eggs, cheese; unhealthy food: crisps, sweets, cakes, chips, fizzy drinks; large poster-size paper; scissors; glue; felt-tip pens

What will the children learn?

◆ Listening and speaking skills – in class discussion and group work
◆ To work as a group
◆ Health and their body
◆ Fine motor skills – cutting and gluing

Group size

Whole class, then small groups

What to do

◆ Show the children different types of food and ask them which they think are healthy and which are unhealthy. Why?
◆ Talk about the terms 'healthy' and 'unhealthy' and discuss why it is important to eat healthy food.
◆ Divide the class into groups of four or five.
◆ Give each group two large sheets of paper and ask them to make two posters: one showing healthy food and one showing unhealthy food.
◆ Provide magazines so that they can cut out pictures. Encourage them to think about the layout of the poster.
◆ Finish by having each group show their work to the rest of the class.

Extension activities

◆ Make some healthy snacks such as a fruit salad to eat at snack time.
◆ Talk about all the people who help keep us healthy: doctors, dentists, opticians, nurses.
◆ Show posters and adverts for healthy foods.
◆ Provide leaflets about healthy eating.
◆ Invite a dietician to come in and talk about healthy eating.

Link to early learning goals

◆ Recognize the importance of keeping healthy and those things which contribute to this

Healthy teeth

You will need
Healthy teeth sheet (see page 163); pieces of small white card; magazines; scissors; glue

Group size
Small groups

What will the children learn?
◆ Good health
◆ Personal hygiene
◆ Independence
◆ Listening and speaking skills – class and group discussion

What to do
◆ Explain to the children that they are going to learn about teeth.
◆ Ask them to point to their teeth and even count them.
◆ Ask them why they think we need teeth. Why is it important to look after them?
◆ Which foods harm teeth? What can they do to look after their teeth?
◆ Give each group of children a photocopy of the Healthy teeth sheet.
◆ Ask them to stick on small pieces of white card for teeth.
◆ Now ask them to cut out pictures from magazines of food that will harm their teeth and stick these on the teeth.
◆ Give them another copy of the sheet and repeat the activity with pictures of food that is good for their teeth.
◆ Compare the two mouths and ask them what will happen to the teeth in each case.

Extension activities
◆ Invite a dentist to come to talk to the children.
◆ Read *Freddie Visits the Dentist* by Nicola Smee (Barrons Educational Series).
◆ Give the children toothbrushes to clean their dolls' teeth.
◆ Put a tooth into a glass of cola and see what happens to it over a period of time.
◆ Talk about the correct way to brush teeth.
◆ Make a bar chart of favourite toothpastes.
◆ Look at the teeth of different animals.

Link to early learning goals
◆ Recognize the importance of keeping healthy and those things which contribute to this

Healthy teeth sheet

Healthy food plate

You will need

Shopping bag containing healthy and unhealthy foods; lunch box containing healthy and unhealthy foods; paper plates; felt-tip pens

Group size

Whole class

What will the children learn?

- Listening and speaking skills – during class discussion
- Sorting skills
- Good health and their bodies
- Creativity and imagination

What to do

- Show the children the shopping bag and ask them to sort the food into two piles: one healthy, the other unhealthy.
- Discuss why some foods are healthy and others are unhealthy. For example, milk is good as it contains calcium to keep bones strong; cola is unhealthy because it contains lots of sugars that cause tooth decay.
- Now show the lunch box and do the same again.
- Give each child a paper plate and on it ask them to draw healthy food that they would like to eat.
- Finish by letting the children show their work to one another. Discuss why the foods they have drawn are healthy.

Extension activities

- Ask the children to show their lunch boxes and discuss what is healthy/unhealthy.
- Stick pictures of healthy food onto card. Laminate and let the children use them as place mats.
- Draw around a pupil to get a body shape. Stick on pictures to show the types of food needed to keep each part of the body healthy; for example, milk for teeth, fruit and vegetables for skin, meat for growth, etc.
- Make a healthy snack such as fruit kebabs (see Fruit kebabs, page 90).

Link to early learning goals

- Recognize the importance of keeping healthy and those things which contribute to this

Going on a Bear Hunt

You will need

Book: *We're Going on a Bear Hunt* by Michael Rosen (Walker Books); mats; apparatus (eg ropes, benches, ladders) set up as for a PE lesson

Group size

Whole class

What to do

- Begin by reading the story *We're Going on a Bear Hunt*.
- Discuss the different ways the characters had to travel: over, under, through.
- Invite the children to act out the story while you read it again.
- Show the children the apparatus.
- Ask them to find as many different ways of travelling over, under, through and around the apparatus.
- Finishing by choosing some children to demonstrate their work.

Extension activities

- Retell the story but change the animal, for example to a tiger.
- Tell the story from the point of view of the bear: I was fast asleep when suddenly ….
- Count how many different ways they can travel on a piece of apparatus.
- Ask the children to suggest different areas that they could go to in the hunt and how they would travel over them. For example, they might scramble over a hill, or walk carefully across a road.

> ## What will the children learn?
> - Gross motor skills
> - Creativity and imagination
> - Words to describe position – 'up', 'over', 'under', etc
> - Opposites – over/under, up/down, etc

> ## Link to early learning goals
> - Travel around, under, over and through balancing and climbing equipment

Grand Old Duke of York

You will need
Two step blocks

Group size
Large groups

What to do
◆ Begin by singing the rhyme 'The Grand Old Duke of York'.
◆ Set up the steps back to back to form a hill.
◆ Explain to the children that they are going to act out the rhyme.
◆ Choose one child to be the Duke.
◆ Ask the Duke to march around. The other children should march behind the Duke and follow him.
◆ Now show them the hill and ask them to march up and down it. They should go up one set of steps and down the other set of steps.
◆ Now sing the song again and ask children to march up and down according to the words of the song.
◆ Let each child have a turn being the Duke.

Extension activities
◆ Make costumes for the Duke and his soldiers.
◆ Decorate the steps so they look like a hill.
◆ Count the number of children and change the song (eg 'The Grand old Duke of York, he had five men…').
◆ Count how many steps there are going up and how many coming down.
◆ Play follow the leader with the children doing different activities, for example balancing on a bench, going through a hoop, going under a rope.

What will the children learn?
◆ To follow the leader and take the lead
◆ Imagination and role play
◆ Gross motor skills – climbing steps using alternate feet
◆ Different ways of travelling – up and down
◆ Opposites – up/down

Link to early learning goals
◆ Travel around, under, over and through balancing and climbing equipment

Clay pot

You will need

Clay; waxed paper; water; aprons; circular cutters; rolling pins; paint; paint brushes

Group size

Small groups

What will the children learn?
- Creativity and imagination
- To use different materials and tools
- Fine motor control

What to do

- Explain to the children that they are going to make a clay pot. Show an example or a picture of one.
- Ask the children to put on aprons.
- Give each child a block of clay on a sheet of waxed paper.
- Ask the children to take a small piece of clay. Show them how to roll it out and cut out a circle using a cutter. This will be the base of the pot.
- Now show the children how to make clay 'sausages' by rolling the clay with the palms of their hands.
- Once they have made enough sausages, show them how to attach them to the base, layer by layer to make a pot shape.
- Show the children how to use water to stick one layer to the next and use their fingers to blend the clay together.
- Ensure the children blend the clay together well or the pot will fall apart when it is baked in the oven.
- Put the finished pots in the oven to bake, following the instructions on the packet.
- Paint the pots and display with a label explaining how they were made.

Extension activities

- Make some others items out of clay such as plates, name labels or pencil holders.
- Make pots using different materials.
- Compare clay when it is dry, wet and baked.
- Count the number of layers in each pot.

Link to early learning goals
- Handle tools, objects, and construction and malleable materials safely and with increasing control

Papier mâché ladybirds

You will need

Pictures of ladybirds; balloons; paste made from flour and water; newspaper torn into strips; plant pots; paint; paint brushes; pipe cleaners; sticky tape

What will the children learn?

◆ Creativity and imagination
◆ To work with a partner – cooperation and sharing
◆ The features of a ladybird
◆ To use a different medium for creative work

Group size

Whole class working in pairs

What to do

◆ Show the children pictures of ladybirds and point out the key features: six legs, oval body, symmetrical pattern of dots on the body.
◆ Divide the children into pairs and give each pair a blown-up balloon. Show them how to wedge it into a plant pot. This will help to keep it steady as they work.
◆ Show the children how to smear the balloon with the flour paste and then stick on newspaper strips. Repeat until the balloon is covered in about three or four layers of paper.
◆ Leave to dry in a warm, dry area.
◆ When the balloon is dry cut it in half and give one half to each child.
◆ Give each child six pipe cleaners to attach as legs to their balloon half.
◆ Paint the ladybirds red or yellow and leave to dry.
◆ Now paint black strip and dots onto the body.
◆ Display all the ladybirds on a background of giant paper leaves.

Extension activities

◆ Read the poem 'Ladybird, Ladybird, Fly Away Home'.
◆ Write a story about a ladybird.
◆ Look for ladybirds in the garden. Where do they live?
◆ Count the dots on a ladybird.
◆ Make an information book about ladybirds: where they live, what they eat, etc.
◆ Read the story *The Bad-Tempered Ladybird* by Eric Carle (Puffin Books).

Link to early learning goals

◆ Handle tools, objects, and construction and malleable materials safely and with increasing control

Personal, Social and Emotional Development

The skills the children learn in this chapter will be valuable to them throughout their lives. It is vital children build a positive attitude to both themselves and others for successful overall development. In this chapter children will have opportunities to:

◆ develop a positive attitude to learning
◆ name and discuss their own feelings and have empathy towards others
◆ encounter and express their feelings in language and through imaginative and creative play
◆ work independently as well as in large and small groups
◆ form good relationships with their peers and adults
◆ accept and work to the rules of the group – turn-taking, sharing, etc
◆ become self-reliant and learn to dress independently
◆ develop self-discipline and moral values
◆ gain confidence and have pride in their achievements
◆ understand they live in a multi-cultural society and must respect and value all people equally.

The early learning goal of Personal, Social and Emotional Development is broken down into 14 learning opportunities, which are listed on the chart on pages 170–171. Each learning opportunity is covered by between two and four activities that will help children achieve that target. The last column on the chart is for comments, and can be used for planning and assessment purposes.

Learning opportunities chart

Learning opportunity	Activities (and page numbers)	Comments
Continue to be interested, excited and motivated to learn	Find the hidden treasure (172); Guess the object (173)	
Be confident to try new activities, initiate ideas and speak in a familiar group	My favourite toy (174); Feel and guess (175); Making puppets (176)	
Maintain attention, concentrate, and sit quietly when appropriate	Sound game (177); Kim's game (178); Praise cards (179)	
Have a developing awareness of their own needs, views and feelings and be sensitive to the needs, views and feelings of others	Happy family book (180); Golden rules (181); Crossing the road (182)	
Have a developing respect for their own cultures and beliefs and those of other people	Special clothes (183); Places of worship (184); Pen pal class (185)	
Respond to significant experiences, showing a range of feelings when appropriate	Happy family book (180); Being new (186)	
Form good relationships with adults and peers	My favourite toy (174); Praise cards (179); Thank you cakes (187–188)	
Work as part of a group or class, taking turns and sharing fairly, understanding that there need to be agreed values and codes of behaviour for groups of people, including adults and children, to work together harmoniously	My favourite toy (174); Golden rules (181); Thank you cakes (187–188); Parachute play (189–190)	
Understand what is right, what is wrong, and why	Golden rules (181); The Boy Who Cried Wolf (191); What is wrong? (192–193)	
Dress and undress independently and manage their own personal hygiene	Special clothes (183); Thank you cakes (187–188); Nursery rhyme dress up (194); Spider perseverance (195–196)	
Select and use activities and resources independently	Making puppets (176); Praise cards (179); Nursery rhyme dress up (194)	

Play Activities for the Early Years
www.brilliantpublications.co.uk

Learning opportunities chart

Learning opportunity	Activities (and page numbers)	Comments
Consider the consequences of their words and actions for themselves and others	Golden rules (181); The Boy Who Cried Wolf (191); Sunflowers (197)	
Understand that people have different needs, views, cultures and beliefs, which need to be treated with respect	Special clothes (183); Places of worship (184); Holiday times (198)	
Understand that they can expect others to treat their needs, views, cultures and beliefs with respect	Pen pal class (185); Festivals (199); All about me (200)	

Find the hidden treasure

You will need

Sand tray full of sand; treasure (brightly coloured buttons, bead necklaces, shiny coins, plastic rings, etc); sieves; colanders; trays; paper; coloured pencils

Group size

Small groups

> ### What will the children learn?
> ◆ That learning is fun and exciting
> ◆ To show curiosity and explore
> ◆ The properties of sand

What to do

- ◆ Hide the treasure in the sand tray.
- ◆ Ask the children to pretend they are searching for hidden treasure.
- ◆ Invite them to look in the sand tray for the treasure.
- ◆ Show the children the different resources they can use to help them in their search (sieves, colanders, etc).
- ◆ When the children have found all the treasure ask them to draw a picture of the things they found.

Extension activities

- ◆ Use water, sawdust or coloured rice instead of sand.
- ◆ Count how many things each child has found.
- ◆ Ask the children to make some treasure to hide.
- ◆ Sort the treasure into hoops – by colour, size, etc.
- ◆ Extend the sand play by giving the children interesting sand equipment such as turning wheels, different size bottles, etc.
- ◆ Read *Spot's Treasure Hunt* by Eric Hill (Putnam Publishing Group).

> ### Link to early learning goals
> ◆ Continue to be interested, excited and motivated to learn

Guess the object

You will need

An unusual item that children are not familiar with, such as an old clothes wringer or washboard

Group size

Large groups

What will the children learn?

◆ To show curiosity and explore
◆ Questioning skills

What to do

◆ Ask the children to sit in a circle.
◆ Show the children the unusual object and pass it round the circle for all the children to examine it in more detail.
◆ Ask the children to guess what it is.
◆ Encourage the children to ask questions.
◆ Finish by revealing what it is.

Extension activities

◆ Ask the children to bring in unusual items from home.
◆ Set up a table with unusual items and a note pad. Let the children explore them during free play and write on the note pad what they think they are.
◆ Ask the children to invent a machine and make it out of junk. Then let other children guess what it is.
◆ Let the children take apart some old items such as watches, clockwork toys, etc.

Link to early learning goals

◆ Continue to be interested, excited and motivated to learn

My favourite toy

You will need

Children to bring in their favourite toy

Group size

Whole class

What to do

- Invite the children to bring in their favourite toy (make sure they are labelled).
- Ask the children to sit in a circle.
- Start by explaining that this session is called circle time and it is a time for the children to sit and talk and listen to one another.
- Explain to the children the two rules important for circle time to ensure it is successful: firstly they must listen to one another, and secondly, they only talk when it is their turn.
- Make sure the children understand the importance and value of the rules.
- Invite the children to show and talk about their favourite toy.
- Once all the children have spoken ask them to swap their toy with the child next to them and play.
- Explain that it is very important that the children take good care of each other's toys.
- Finish the activity by returning the toys to their owner.

What will the children learn?

- Listening and speaking skills – during class discussion
- Group cooperation and to trust in one another
- To share and take turns
- To put their views across and talk freely about something personal to themselves
- To take an interest in others
- The importance of rules

Extension activities

- Circle time could be used for all types of topics.
- Make a book of favourites: favourite food, favourite book, favourite lesson, etc.
- Make up a story about their toy.
- Sort toys into hoops – by colour, shape, etc.
- Share different things between the children such as food at snack time.

Links to early learning goals

- Be confident to try new activities, initiate ideas and speak in a familiar group
- Form good relationships with adults and peers
- Work as part of a group or class, taking turns and sharing fairly, understanding that there need to be agreed values and codes of behaviour for groups of people, including adults and children, to work harmoniously

Feel and guess

You will need
A bag with a drawstring; different items for children to fool (eg soft teddy bear, wooden spoon, key, pine cone)

Group size
Small groups

What will the children learn?
◆ To investigate and explore
◆ To develop their tactile ability
◆ To develop concentration and vocabulary
◆ To listen and speak in a small group

What to do
◆ Show children the bag and explain that you would like them to take turns and feel the object inside and guess what it is.
◆ Let the children take turns. Ask questions and encourage them to talk as much as they can about what they feel.
◆ Ask the children not to guess what it is until everyone has had their turn to feel the object.
◆ Finish by letting the children guess what it could be, then reveal what it actually is.
◆ Do the same with the other objects.

Extension activities
◆ Adapt the game by blindfolding children and asking them to feel bowls of different items such as jelly, pasta, sawdust and rice.
◆ Make the game harder by giving objects which are similar to one another (eg the same shape – coins, buttons, washers, counters).
◆ Blindfold a child and ask them to feel another child's face and guess who it is.
◆ Place unusual objects into the bag.
◆ Instead of a feely bag make a feely box by taking a shoe box and putting a hole in the lid. Place an object inside. Let the children put their hand through the hole to feel.

Link to early learning goals
◆ Be confident to try new activities, initiate ideas and speak in a familiar group

Making puppets

You will need

Pictures and books about puppets; socks; buttons; string; paper bags; wooden spoons; fabric bits; wool; glue; sticky tape; junk materials; scissors; paint; paint brushes

Group size

Small groups

What will the children learn?

◆ Creativity and imagination
◆ To share ideas
◆ To work independently

What to do

◆ Show the children books and pictures of different types of puppets.
◆ If possible take the children to see a puppet show or invite a puppet show to the school.
◆ Show the children the resources and discuss with them how they could make a puppet with the resources available. Let the children share their ideas.
◆ Invite the children to make their own puppets. Ask them to select their resources and allow them to work as independently as possible.
◆ Finish by letting the children show their puppets to their peers and explain how they made them. Ask questions to encourage them to tell the rest of the group as much as possible.

Extension activities

◆ Use the puppets to make a puppet show (see Puppet theatre, page 33).
◆ Make up stories for the puppets to act out.
◆ Use puppets to discuss emotions.
◆ Retell stories using puppets.

Links to early learning goals

◆ Be confident to try new activities, initiate ideas and speak in a familiar group
◆ Select and use activities and resources independently

Sound game

You will need

Different objects that make sounds (eg clocks, musical instruments, spoons, wind chimes, bells, etc)

Group size

Whole class

What will the children learn?

◆ Listening and concentration skills
◆ To identify sounds
◆ To take turns

What to do

◆ Begin by sitting all the children in a circle.
◆ Show each of the objects and demonstrate the sound it makes.
◆ Encourage the children to sit quietly and concentrate.
◆ Now choose one child to close their eyes and another child to choose an object and make the sound.
◆ The first child then guesses what the object is.
◆ Repeat the activity so that each child gets to have a turn at guessing.

Extension activities

◆ Clap a pattern and ask children to repeat it back using one of the objects.
◆ Ask the children to use objects to make music.
◆ Make up a short poem about things that make a noise. For example:

   The clock goes tick, tock,
   The bell goes ting-a-ling.

◆ Read the story *Peace at Last* by Jill Murphy (Macmillan Children's Books).

Link to early learning goals

◆ Maintain attention, concentrate, and sit quietly when appropriate

Kim's game

You will need
Tray of different items (eg clock, pen, key, ball); cloth to cover tray; flip chart; pen

Group size
Large groups

What will the children learn?
- To increase their concentration span
- To pay attention
- To develop visual memory skills

What to do
- Explain to the children that they are going to play Kim's game, a game where they must really concentrate and use their memory.
- Show them the tray of objects covered by the cloth.
- Explain to the children that you are going to uncover the tray for just a short period of time.
- In that time the children must look and try to remember the objects on the tray.
- Remove the cloth for about a minute and then cover up again.
- Ask the children to tell you what was on the tray, and write their guesses on a flip chart.
- Uncover the tray and see if they were right.

Extension activities
- Start off with just three objects and then increase the number to make it harder.
- Make the game harder by asking children to remember not only the objects but also their position on the tray.
- Count how many items are on the tray.
- Use objects that look similar to make the game more challenging.

Link to early learning goals
- Maintain attention, concentrate and sit quietly when appropriate

Praise cards

You will need
Small cards with names of all the children in the class; bag; card; felt-tip pens; glitter; sticky paper; fabric bits; stars; glue

Group size
Whole class

What will the children learn?
- Listening and speaking skills – during circle time
- Self-esteem – receiving praise from their peers
- Social skills

What to do
- Place all the card names inside the a bag and shake.
- Ask the children to sit in a circle.
- Ask each child to pick a name from the bag.
- Going round in a circle, ask each to say what they like about the person whose name they picked.
- Invite the children to make a card for that person using the variety of resources available. Allow them to work as independently as possible.
- Finish the activity by having each child give and receive a card.

Extension activities
- Ask the children to work together on other activities (eg reading a book together).
- Invite the children to share toys with each other (see My favourite toy, page 174).
- Share food at snack time (see International food, page 128).
- Pair children up and ask them to find out as much about each other as possible and then ask them to make a book about each other.

Links to early learning goals
- Maintain attention, concentrate, and sit quietly when appropriate
- Form good relationships with adults and peers
- Select and use activities and resources independently

Happy family book

You will need

Empty workbooks (or sheets of blank paper stapled together to make a book); crayons, pens, etc

Group size

Whole class, then small groups

What will the children learn?
- ◆ Listening and speaking skills – in class discussion
- ◆ To express feelings and emotions
- ◆ To understand the feelings and views of others
- ◆ To view differences and similarities between people

What to do

- ◆ Begin by discussing the term 'happiness'. Ask the children to talk about what makes them happy.
- ◆ Give each child a workbook and ask them to draw a picture of themselves and what makes them happy on the first page.
- ◆ On the other pages ask them to draw other members of their family.
- ◆ Now ask the children to take the book home and ask their family members to draw what makes them happy next to their picture.
- ◆ When the books are returned to school, put the children into groups and ask them to discuss the different things they found that made different people happy.
- ◆ Encourage them to listen carefully to one another.
- ◆ Display the books in the book corner for children to share.

Extension activities

- ◆ Do the same activity but with a different emotion.
- ◆ Make happy and sad masks (see Happy/sad masks, pages 22–24).
- ◆ Make a book about feelings. Start each page: I am happy when… I am angry when… I am excited when…, etc.
- ◆ Sing the song 'If You're Happy and You Know It Clap Your Hands'.
- ◆ Do actions to express emotions. For example, if they are pretending to be angry they might stamp their feet (see Feeling faces, pages 141–142).

Links to early learning goals
- ◆ Have a developing awareness of their own needs, views and feelings and be sensitive to the needs, views and feelings of others
- ◆ Respond to significant experiences, showing a range of feelings when appropriate

Golden rules

You will need
Flip chart and felt-tip pens; golden pen

Group size
Whole class

What will the children learn?
◆ Speaking and listening – in class discussions
◆ To voice their needs and listen to others
◆ The importance of self-control and self-discipline
◆ To understand what rules are and their purpose

What to do
◆ Begin by asking the children to talk about how they would like their classroom to be for them to learn. Encourage them to discuss their needs.
◆ Explain the term 'rules'.
◆ Invite the children to think of some rules that everybody must adhere to.
◆ Encourage the children to express their views in turn and to listen carefully to each other's views. Encourage debate.
◆ Write down all the suggestions on paper.
◆ With the children, select the best five.
◆ Write these down with a golden pen and call them the golden rules.
◆ Emphasize that these rules need to be adhered to by everyone in the class.
◆ Also discuss the consequences if one of the rules is broken and decide what will happen as a result.
◆ Finish by displaying the golden rules in a prominent place.

Extension activities
◆ Talk about rules in different places and their purpose, for example the rules of the road, rules at home.
◆ Give rewards to children who follow the rules.
◆ Go on a trip and discuss how the children must behave so that everybody is safe.
◆ Invite some speakers to the class. Beforehand discuss with the children how they must behave and treat the visitors.

Links to early learning goals
◆ Have a developing awareness of their own needs, views and feelings and be sensitive to the needs, views and feelings of others
◆ Work as part of a group or class, taking turns and sharing fairly, understanding that there need to be agreed values and codes of behaviour for groups of people, including adults and children, to work harmoniously
◆ Understand what is right, what is wrong, and why
◆ Consider the consequences of their words and actions for themselves and others

Crossing the road

You will need

An area of playground marked out as a road (include zebra crossing and traffic lights); play cars, bicycles and tricycles

Group size

Large groups

What will the children learn?
◆ Road safety
◆ How to keep themselves safe
◆ The needs of pedestrians and drivers
◆ Role play

What to do

◆ Talk to the children about how they cross roads. Discuss where is it safe to cross. Why do they need to take care?

◆ Go through the basic rules: always hold an adult's hand, stand on the pavement in a safe place, continue to look and listen when crossing.

◆ Now talk to the children about the rules and needs of drivers. For example, they need to obey the speed limit, look out for pedestrians, stop at zebra crossings.

◆ Show the children the road area outside.

◆ Ask some children to be the pedestrians and some to be the drivers.

◆ Remind the pedestrians that they need to cross the road safely and the drivers that they need to drive carefully and look out for pedestrians.

◆ Model how you would like the children to behave: hold the children's hands and cross at the zebra crossing, pretend to drive a car and stop at the traffic lights.

◆ Let all the children have turns being both a driver and a pedestrian.

Extension activities

◆ Invite a policeman to come in and talk about road safety.

◆ Talk to children about how they can keep safe in different circumstances: when near a river or pond, when out in a large shopping centre, etc.

◆ Provide police men/women and lollipop people dressing-up clothes.

◆ Talk about the Green Cross Code. Encourage the children to memorize it.

Link to early learning goals
◆ Have a developing awareness of their own needs, views and feelings and be sensitive to the needs, views and feelings of others

Special clothes

You will need
Dressing-up clothes and hats from around the world: saris – India, salwar kameez – Pakistan, kimono – Japan, grass skirts – Hawaii; pictures and books of people in different national costumes

Group size
Whole class, then small groups

What to do
- Show pictures and books of people in different national costumes.
- Show the different items of dressing-up clothes and introduce the correct names.
- Encourage the children to touch the different items and to ask questions.
- Now let the children dress up in the clothes using pictures as a guide. Give help when needed.
- Finish by letting the children show their costumes to the rest of the class. Encourage them to talk about which country an item of clothing comes from and its name. For example: 'I am wearing a sari from India.'

Extension activities
- Invite adults from different communities to show how to put on different clothing and help the children to dress up.
- Read the book *Children Just Like Me* by Barnabas and Anabel Kindersley (Dorling Kindersley Publishing).
- Ask the children to bring in some special clothing from home.
- Use different fabrics and patterns to make an international quilt.
- Ask parents to make child-sized international clothing for the home corner.
- Look closely at the patterns on saris. Try to copy them.

What will the children learn?
- To recognize and name items of clothing from around the world
- To dress up independently
- To respect people's cultures

Links to early learning goals
- Have a developing respect for their own cultures and beliefs and those of other people
- Dress and undress independently and manage their own personal hygiene
- Understand that people have different needs, views, cultures and beliefs, which need to be treated with respect

Places of worship

You will need
Pictures, books, videos of different places of worship (church, mosque, synagogue, etc); camera; paper; pencils; clipboards; people from different communities

Group size
Whole class

What to do
◆ Organize a trip to different places of worship (if possible try to cover most of the different religions of the children in the class).
◆ Show pictures and/or videos of the places before going.
◆ Prepare the children in advance. Remind them they must respect other people's beliefs and customs (cover their head, remove their shoes, etc).
◆ During the trip take some photographs and back at school ask children to draw pictures of the things they liked.
◆ Invite some people from different communities to visit the class.
◆ Prepare questions in advance and encourage the children to be respectful and listen attentively.
◆ Finish by displaying the photos and pictures of the trip.

Extension activities
◆ Show artefacts from different places of worship.
◆ Make stained glass windows and other relevant artwork (see Stained glass pictures, page 140).
◆ Talk about and celebrate different festivals: Hanukkah, Eid, Diwali, Holi.
◆ Make a journal of their various visits.
◆ Show children scripts in various languages (see Books from around the world, page 50).
◆ Listen to religious songs in different languages.

Links to early learning goals
◆ Have a developing respect for their own cultures and beliefs and those of other people
◆ Understand that people have different needs, views, cultures and beliefs, which need to be treated with respect

Pen pal class

You will need
Large sheet of paper; pen; envelope; stamp; books about country where pen pal class is based

Group size
Whole class

What will the children learn?
◆ Listening and speaking skills – in class discussions
◆ Letter-writing
◆ To develop an understanding of different countries and cultures
◆ To see similarities and differences between themselves and other children around the world

What to do
◆ Make contact with a school abroad and choose a class with which your class can be pen pals.
◆ Talk to the class about the class abroad and read some books about the country they are in.
◆ Ask the children to decide what they would like to write to the class and scribe a letter on a large sheet of paper.
◆ Encourage children to provide information about themselves and also to think about specific questions they would like to have answered.
◆ Now mail the letter to the other class. If possible include some photos and pictures the children have made.
◆ The recipient class and teacher can then respond in a similar fashion.
◆ A relationship is now formed where both classes can learn about each other.

Extension activities
◆ Do a teacher swap.
◆ Made a tape recording of the children's ideas and views to send to the pen pal class.
◆ If possible use a computer so children can e-mail one another.
◆ Make a reference book about the country.
◆ Make a class book with the children's pictures and information about themselves.
◆ As the children get older allocate each one an individual pen pal.

Links to early learning goals
◆ Have a developing respect for their own cultures and beliefs and those of other people
◆ Understand that they can expect others to treat their needs, views, cultures and beliefs with respect

Being new

You will need

Book: *Blue Horse and Tilly* by Helen Stephens (Scholastic)

Group size

Whole class, then in pairs

What to do

- Read the story *Blue Horse and Tilly*.
- Talk about the story and how Tilly felt shy when she moved to her new house.
- Ask if any of the children have moved house. How did they feel?
- Ask the children to think how they could welcome a new child to their class. For example, they might ask them their name, introduce themselves, ask them to play.
- Pair children and ask one child to be the new child and the other to be the welcomer. Invite them to role play what they might say and do.
- Now ask the children to swap roles and play again.
- Finish by letting the children talk about their role play and about the different things they did to welcome the newcomer.

What will the children learn?

- To understand their own feelings and those of others
- To empathize with others
- Listening and speaking skills – in class discussion and whilst working in pairs
- Role play
- Group cooperation

Extension activities

- Use puppets to discuss feelings and different scenarios.
- Talk about different feelings (happiness, sadness, etc), and ask the children to relate it to their own lives.
- Read the story *Can't You Sleep, Little Bear?* by Martin Waddell (Walker Books) and ask children to think about times when they were scared.
- Use other storybooks to raise discussions about feelings.

Link to early learning goals

- Respond to significant experiences, showing a range of feelings when appropriate

186
Play Activities for the Early Years
www.brilliantpublications.co.uk

Thank you cakes

You will need
Recipe for thank you cakes (see page 188); ingredients and equipment as specified on recipe sheet

Group size
Small groups

What will the children learn?
- To appreciate other people
- To discuss emotions
- Listening and speaking skills – class discussion
- Science of cooking – change in the ingredients
- Group cooperation and taking turns
- Personal hygiene

What to do
- Explain to the children that, as a group, they are going to make some 'thank you' cakes
- Ask each child to think of someone they would like to give the cakes to and why. Offer suggestions (secretary, lollypop person, caretaker, etc).
- Talk about the importance of good hygiene when cooking and ask the children to wash their hands, put on an apron and tie back their hair. Let them do this as independently as possible.
- Make the cakes as shown on the recipe sheet.
- Ask the children to invite the person they have chosen to the classroom to give them the cake.
- Finish by letting the children present the cake to the person they want to say thank you to.
- Sit together as a group and share the cakes.

Extension activities
- Make thank you cards to go with the cakes.
- Do some more cooking: pizzas, salads.
- Design and make some packaging for the cakes.
- Count how many cakes are made.

Links to early learning goals
- Form good relationships with adults and peers
- Work as part of a group or class, taking turns and sharing fairly, understanding that there need to be agreed values and codes of behaviour for groups of people, including adults and children, to work together harmoniously
- Dress and undress independently and manage their own personal hygiene

Recipe for thank you cakes

Ingredients

100 g (4 oz) flour

100 g (4 oz) softened butter

100 g (4 oz) sugar

2 small eggs

To decorate the cakes

icing

hundreds and thousands

Equipment

bowl

spoon

baking tray

oven

paper cake cases

What to do

✳ Preheat the oven to 180°C/350°F, gas mark 4.

✳ Start by showing the ingredients.

✳ Help the children to weigh them and put all the ingredients in a bowl.

✳ Now stir the mixture. Allow all the children to do this in turn.

✳ Place the paper cases on the baking tray and ask the children to take turns to pour the mixture into the cases.

✳ Place in the oven for 15–20 minutes.

✳ Once baked and cooled allow the children to decorate the cakes as they wish.

188 **Play Activities for the Early Years**
www.brilliantpublications.co.uk

Parachute play

You will need
Parachute games sheet (see page 190); parachute; sponge balls; different coloured bean bags; two adult helpers

Group size
Whole class

What will the children learn?
◆ To work together and to trust one another
◆ Listening skills – following and understanding instructions
◆ Cooperation
◆ Gross motor control

What to do
◆ Explain to the children that they are going to play some games using the parachute.
◆ With the adult helpers spread out the parachute on the floor.
◆ Ask the children to sit just beyond the edge of the parachute but not to touch it.
◆ Space the adults evenly between the children.
◆ Before playing explain to the children that they need to listen very carefully and work together for the games to work successfully.
◆ Ask the children to kneel and hold the parachute in their hands.
◆ Now ask them to stand up.
◆ Begin by asking the children to slowly raise the parachute up and down. Help them to get used to the idea of playing with it.
◆ Play some of the games on the Parachute games sheet.
◆ Whilst the children are playing remind them to carry on listening carefully and working together.
◆ Finish the session by doing activity 5 or 6 on the sheet.

Extension activities
◆ Ask the children to make up some games they can play with the parachute.
◆ Use the parachute for drama work and with songs.
◆ Use the parachute as a tent and have story time sitting on it (see Parachute games sheet).
◆ Ask the children to work together for other activities such as painting a picture, building a model.
◆ Invite the children to make some food and share at snack time.

Link to early learning goals
◆ Work as part of a group or class, taking turns and sharing fairly, understanding that there need to be agreed values and codes of behaviour for groups of people, including adults and children, to work together harmoniously

Parachute games

1. Ask the children to pretend that the parachute is water. Start by keeping the parachute still like calm water in a pond, then move the parachute to form ripples, now raise it up and down to form waves. Finish by shaking it fast like a storm.

2. Throw a sponge ball onto the parachute. Ask the children to move the ball around but try not to let it fall off.

3. Keep the ball on the parachute, and ask children to throw the ball up as high as they can.

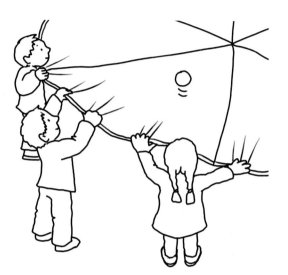

4. Put a couple of balls on the parachute. Ask the children to shake and bounce the balls.

5. Ask the children to pull the parachute over their heads and sit on it – like a tent. This is a good way to have quiet time.

6. Ask some children to lie under the parachute whilst the rest of the class raises it up and down to create a relaxing breeze.

7. Play games where some children run under the parachute while the rest of the group supports it. You could place some different coloured bean bags under the parachute. Choose children to go under the parachute to get a particular bean bag: 'Sophie, can you get me a green bean bag.?'

8. Repeat 7 but add different equipment such as quoits. You can make it more difficult by asking children to bring out two items: 'Sunil, can you get me the red bean bag and the yellow quoit.?'

The Boy Who Cried Wolf

You will need
Book: *The Boy Who Cried Wolf*, flip chart and pens

Group size
Whole class

What will the children learn?
- Listening and speaking skills – in class discussion
- Social skills
- The importance of telling the truth
- To retell a story

What to do
- Begin by reading the story *The Boy Who Cried Wolf*.
- Discuss the story. Why didn't anybody listen to the boy anymore? Why should the boy have told the truth?
- Discuss the term 'honesty' and what it means. Help the children relate it to their own lives.
- As a class retell the story, but this time the boy tells the truth. Scribe the story on a flip chart.

Extension activities
- Play a true or false game.
- Teach other values: respect, self-control, courage, etc.
- Read other books with similar themes.
- Watch the film *Pinocchio* (Walt Disney).

Links to early learning goals
- Understand what is right, what is wrong, and why
- Consider the consequences of their words and actions for themselves and others

What is wrong?

You will need

What is wrong? picture sheet
(see page 193)

Group size

Large groups

What to do

◆ Show the children the picture sheet.
◆ Look at picture 1. Ask the children what the child is doing wrong and why it is wrong. (The child is throwing rubbish on the floor – this makes the area very untidy and unhealthy.)
◆ Ask how the child could correct his mistake (eg put the rubbish in the bin).
◆ Now look at and discuss the other pictures on the sheet.

Extension activities

◆ Discuss each action in more depth and relate it to the children's lives. How can we have a cleaner playground, how do we cross a road safely, etc?
◆ Think about and disucss other wrong actions for example not listening to others.
◆ Make a list of class rules (see Golden rules, page 181).
◆ Give stickers/certificates to reward very good behaviour and major achievements (see Good manners certificate, pages 35–36).
◆ Make up a story about someone who does something wrong. Ask the children to finish the story.

Link to early learning goals
◆ Understand what is right, what is wrong, and why;

What is wrong? picture sheet

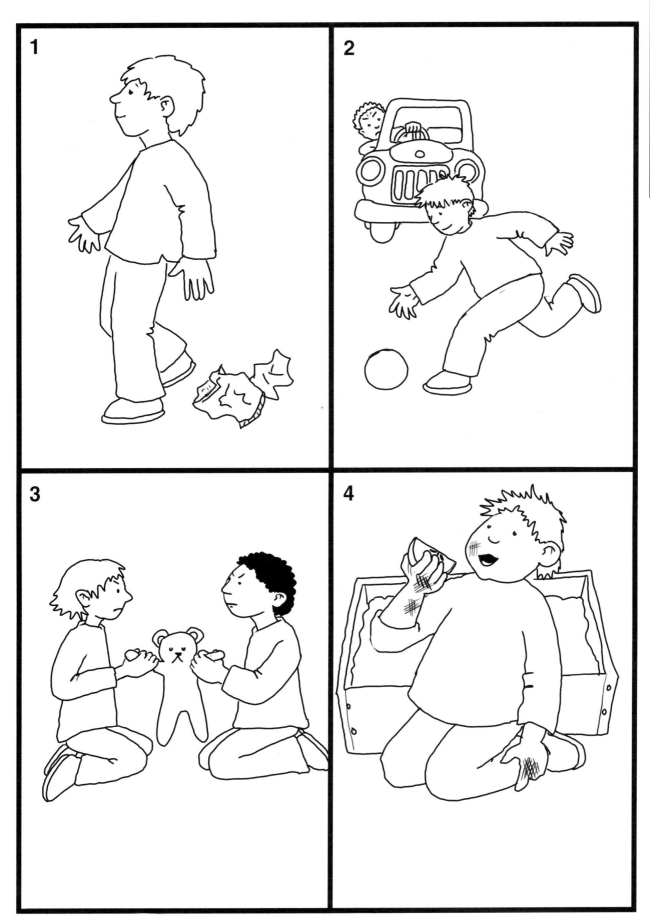

Nursery rhyme dress up

You will need

A variety of dressing-up clothes and props; nursery rhyme books

Group size

Whole class, then small groups

What will the children learn?

◆ To recite nursery rhymes from memory
◆ Role play – different nursery rhyme characters
◆ Independence – to dress themselves

What to do

◆ Begin by reading some well-known nursery rhymes such as 'Humpty Dumpty', 'Jack and Jill'.
◆ Show the children the dressing-up clothes.
◆ Divide the children into groups of two or three and give each group one nursery rhyme.
◆ Ask the children to play dressing up with the clothes and act out the nursery rhyme. Let them dress up independently.
◆ Finish by letting each group act out their rhyme for the rest of the class.

Extension activities

◆ Perform the rhymes in assembly or for other groups of children.
◆ Play an I Spy rhyming game: 'I spy something that rhymes with "cat"' (see I Spy rhyming game, page 14).
◆ Make some props in art work. For example, you could make a Humpty Dumpty by covering a balloon with papier mâché.
◆ Sequence pictures of nursery rhymes (see Nursery rhymes, pages 16–17).
◆ Let the children make up their own rhymes and record these on a tape.

Links to early learning goals
◆ Dress and undress independently and manage their own personal hygiene
◆ Select and use activities and resources independently

Spider perseverance

You will need
Book: *The Very Busy Spider* by Eric Carle (Hamish Hamilton Children's Books); children's coat; The story of Robert the Bruce and the spider (see page 196)

Group size
Whole class

What will the children learn?
◆ Listening and speaking during class discussion
◆ To understand the term 'perseverance' and relate it to themselves
◆ Independence
◆ To take pride in their own achievements

What to do
◆ Begin by reading the story *The Very Busy Spider*.
◆ Discuss the story and ask the children why they think the spider kept on working really hard to finish his web.
◆ Talk about the legend of Robert the Bruce and the spider (see page 196).
◆ Introduce the word 'perseverance' and explain what it means – to keep on trying to do something until it is achieved.
◆ Ask the children to think of situations in which they have persevered, for example tying their shoelaces, learning to ride a bike, learning to cut up their food by themselves.
◆ Ask them to think about how they felt when they had to keep on trying and how they felt when they accomplished it.
◆ Now ask the children to try to put on their coat by themselves.
◆ Emphasize that it is a hard task but they must persevere.
◆ Praise the children for their efforts.

Extension activities
◆ Do the same activity but ask children to tie their shoelaces or change their clothes for PE.
◆ Talk about how sports stars have to practise over and over again.
◆ Make an achievement book where children can write down all they things they have mastered.
◆ Count the number of pieces of clothing they have to take off and put on for a PE lesson.
◆ Play dressing up in the home corner.
◆ Read the book *I Wish I Could Count to a Million* by Joyce Dunbar (Hodder and Stoughton Children's Division).

Link to early learning goals
◆ Dress and undress independently

The story of Robert the Bruce and the spider

Hundreds of years ago Scotland had a king and his name was Robert the Bruce. He was a brave and wise king, but he lived in dangerous times. The king of England wanted to take over Scotland and make it part of England. Many times the great army of England fought against Robert and his small army. Robert and his army fought hard but they were beaten down at each hurdle. Finally Robert and his men were forced to flee.

Robert ran into the wood and hid in a cave. He was tired and sad and wanted to give up the fight. Whilst lying there he noticed a spider weaving its web. He watched as the spider wove its web slowly and carefully, but every time the web was nearly finished a gust of wind would break it down. Each time this happended the spider would start again to weave its web and each time the web was almost finished it would be broken. 'You, too, know what it's like to fail,' thought Robert.

But the spider did not give up. On its tenth attempt the spider succeeded in completing its web. Robert let out a shout of joy! He now knew he could not give up and he gathered his men to fight one more great battle. This time Robert and his army won and the king of England and his army were forced back to their own country.

Robert never forgot the spider and how it inspired him to his victory.

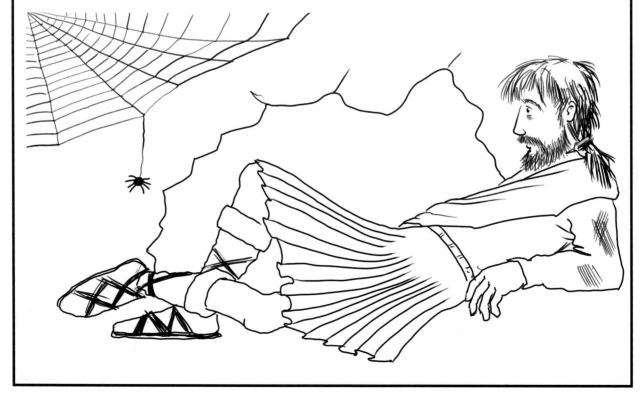

Play Activities for the Early Years
www.brilliantpublications.co.uk

Sunflowers

You will need
Empty pots; soil; sunflower seeds; water; watering cans

Group size
Pairs

> ## What will the children learn?
> ◆ To work as a pair – cooperation, sharing and turn-taking
> ◆ To show care for and look after living things
> ◆ To take on responsibility
> ◆ To see the consequences of their actions

What to do
◆ Divide the children into pairs.
◆ Explain to the children that they are going to plant some sunflower seeds to make the outdoor area look nice.
◆ Give each pair a pot. Ask them to put in some soil, place in the seeds and then cover with some more soil.
◆ Water and explain to the children that it is now their responsibility to water the pots regularly.
◆ Explain that the seeds will not survive without water, but that too much water is also bad.
◆ Encourage the children to decide which one of them is going to water and when.
◆ Point out that plants also need sunlight to grow so the children must decide on the best place to put their pot.
◆ Now leave the children to look after their plant.
◆ After two weeks check which plants have grown. If some have not grown, ask the children why.

Extension activities
◆ Ask the children to plant some cress seeds in order to make sandwiches for lunch time – if they don't grow any, then they won't be able to make cress sandwiches.
◆ Invite the children to look after the class pet.
◆ Observe some minibeasts. Ensure the children understand how to pick them up and handle them carefully.
◆ Talk about how the children look after any pets they have at home.
◆ Discuss the things plants need to grow (see My own garden, page 104).
◆ Read the book *Daisy's Giant Sunflower* by Emma Damon (Tango Books).

> ## Link to early learning goals
> ◆ Consider the consequences of their words and actions for themselves and others

Holiday times

You will need

Map of the world; reference books about different countries; children from an older class

Group size

Whole class, then in pairs

What to do

What will the children learn?

◆ Listening and speaking skills – during group discussion and also in pairs
◆ Country names and location on world map
◆ Information about another country – culture, customs, etc
◆ Group cooperation – sharing books, reading together, sharing information

◆ Begin by discussing holidays and the different countries the children have visited.
◆ Show the children a world map and discuss the colours: blue is for water and green is for land.
◆ Explain to the children that they are going to pretend that the whole class is going on holiday.
◆ Ask one child to point to a green area and read out the name of the country. This is the holiday destination.
◆ Ask the children what they already know about that country.
◆ Pair the children with children from an older class.
◆ Ask the older children to find and read books about that country to the younger children.
◆ Encourage the children to find out specific things such as what language is spoken there, what the weather is like, interesting places to see and different customs.
◆ Now discuss in a group the information the children found out.

Extension activities

◆ Make a class book about the country.
◆ Have a country day. The children can dress in the traditional clothes of the country, listen to music, eat traditional food, etc.
◆ Cook a dish from the country, for example pizza from Italy, paella from Spain, chapattis from India (see International food, pages 128–129).
◆ Make a bar chart showing the number of children who have visited various countries.
◆ Set up chairs like the inside of an aeroplane and role play going on holiday.

Link to early learning goals

◆ Understand that people have different needs, views, cultures and beliefs, which need to be treated with respect

Festivals

You will need
No special requirements

Group size
Whole class

What to do
◆ Talk to children about
   Christmas time and how it is a festival celebrated by Christians around the world.
◆ Ask the children if they celebrate any other festivals.
◆ Encourage the children to talk about the festivals they celebrate and encourage the rest of the group to ask questions such as: When is it celebrated? What special things do you do?
◆ Insist that the children listen carefully and show respect to the child who is speaking.
◆ Make a list of the festivals.
◆ Choose a festival to research further each term.

Extension activities
◆ Invite people from other cultures to come in and speak to the children about the festivals they celebrate.
◆ Invite the children to bring in pictures or artefacts to do with the festival.
◆ Have a festival party.
◆ Learn different festival greetings, for example to wish someone a happy Eid is 'Eid Mubarak'.
◆ Learn how to say hello and goodbye in different languages.
◆ Show children some dual-language books.
◆ Read *The Festival* by Peter Bonnici (Carolrhada Books) and *Samira's Eid* by Nasreen Aktar (Mantra Publishing).

What will the children learn?
◆ Different cultures and festivals
◆ To treat others with respect
◆ To trust others will treat them with respect
◆ Listening and speaking skills – talk about their festival, ask questions, and listen to others

---

Link to early learning goals
◆ Understand that they can expect others to treat their needs, views, cultures and beliefs with respect

All about me

You will need
Microphone

Group size
Whole class

What to do

◆ Ask the children to sit in a circle.
◆ Show the children the microphone and point out that the children can only talk if they are holding it.
◆ Begin the activity by introducing yourself and saying a few words about yourself. For example, 'I am Mrs Patel, I am 30 years old, I am Indian, my favourite colour is yellow.'
◆ Now pass on the microphone to the child sitting beside you and invite him or her to say their name and a few words about themselves (how old they are, who is in their family, which religion they are, etc).
◆ Explain that when one child is speaking the other children must treat them with respect and listen carefully.
◆ Allow everybody to have a turn. Finish the activity by asking some questions to see if they have been listening carefully. Who can remember what David's favourite colour was? How old is Emily?

Extension activities
◆ Invite the children to make a book about themselves.
◆ Circle time is ideal to carry out other discussion work.
◆ Ask the children to work with their best friend and then make a book about them.
◆ Make a class year book with one page for each child. Include a photograph of the child and help them write a small autobiography.
◆ Ask the children to record a little about themselves onto a tape recorder.
◆ Read *All About Me* (Dorling Kindersley Publishing).

Link to early learning goals
◆ Understand that they can expect others to treat their needs, views, cultures and beliefs with respect